W9-ATL-198

THE WORLD'S BEST
SHORT STORIES

127 FUNNY SHORT STORIES
ABOUT UNBELIEVABLE STUFF
THAT ACTUALLY HAPPENED

BILL O'NEILL

ISBN: 978-1-64845-110-2

Copyright © 2023 by LAK Publishing

ALL RIGHTS RESERVED

No part of this book may be reproduced, stored in a retrieval
system, or transmitted in any form or by any means, electronic,
mechanical, photocopying, recording, scanning, or otherwise,
without the prior written permission of the publisher.

CONTENTS

Introduction 1

Guerrilla Warfare Against Flightless Birds 3

"I Can't Go When Watched!" 5

Carrot Subterfuge 7

Bizarre Food Origins 9

The Pains and Struggles of Winning the Lottery 11

The Silent Criminal 13

How Do They Catch It? 15

A Sword Atop the Mountain 16

A Nice Nazi Is Still A Nazi 18

The Habits of Nikola Tesla, Nikola Tesla, Nikola Tesla 20

"Hey Alexa! Butt Out Of My Relationship!" 21

Watch Out! That's The Emancipator's Music! 23

Are You Going To Eat With That? 25

Honey Come Closer, The Flies Are Hungry 27

That Would Hurt A Choco-LOT! 28

You're Not Leaving This Table Until You're Seeing Double! 30

No one's Taking That Record From Her 32

"I'm More of a God Guy" 34

"He's Not The Most Social Chap" 36

Bunnies: Fighting Bullies since 1807 38

Heroin: The Original Cough Medicine 40

Pet tu Brutus? 42

The First Man-Powered Alarm Clocks...44

Lost in Translation 46

Who Won The Art-thletics This Year?..48

When Will the Age of the Silver Fox Begin? 50

Fly With The Angels 52

Bad Luck to Bring a Woman Onboard, Unless You're This Woman ... 54

St. Louis Marathon Mishaps 56

Furious WidowsMake Great Soldiers 59

Someone's Got A Case Of The Mondays!..61

The San Diego Rainmaker 63

The Gift of 10 Million Women 65

Sometimes You Just Yearn for a Babybel..67

The Goldfish Gulping Fad of 1939 69

The Egyptian Pregnancy Test 71

The 66 CE Mooning 73

So, Howl Do I Sign Up? 75

Imagine The Hangover… 77

It's Cheap as Chimps to Employ Him 78

Mid-Life Crisis: Red Ferrari Or Plunderin' Booty? 80

Hide and Don't Go Seek 82

"Houston, Do You Copy?" "…woof" 84

"I Do Hope We Didn't Miss Anything Important" 86

The Best Worst Job In All The Land...88

Who Wants Seconds? 90

Too Delicious For Their Own Good...91

The Worst Thing Since Non-Sliced Bread 93

Do We Name It Cornhub?..95

DON'T FORGET:
TWO FREE BOOKS

GET THEM FOR FREE ON
WWW.TRIVIABILL.COM

Oliver "Scrooge McGrinch" Cromwell 192

The Spaghettree 193

A Place to Pay Your Res-poo-cts...194

"I Apologize Profusely for Doing Exactly as Asked" 195

Stop, Think, and Stop Again, Then Look, Then Stop 197

Introducing Admiral Dr Pepper and Captain Fanta.........................199

What do They Plan on Doing With it?..201

We Had Your Cake and Ate It. Sorry. 203

We Didn't Mean Unlimited! We Meant "Unlimited"! 205

Ariana Grande's BBQ Finger and Grill 207

Maybe Sharknado Isn't That Unrealistic...209

Get That Monkey Some Trousers! And Where's the Llama's
Diaper? 211

13 Yule Lads 213

The Great Lute Defense 215

Hilarious! You're Killing Me! 217

If Only There Was a Hydrant Nearby 218

Someone in Here is a Spy, Any Ideas? 220

The Masked Marauders 222

You Really are Quite the ASSASSIN, aren't you? 224

And There's No Big Hat Emporium Around Here?...........................226

The Poetry of Mrs. Silence Dogood...228

Around the World in 169 Days...230

You Have the Right to Remain Silent. Which You're Doing
Very Well. 232

Agent Snuggles, Reporting For Milk — I Mean Duty 234

Boris Yeltsin's Late-Night Pizza 236

Conclusion 237

Did You Vote For Him? Did Anyone? 143

Why Avoid a Curry Before the Big Game 145

If They Find Out, They'll Erect Statues in my Honor 147

The Salem Tomato Trials 149

A Tsunami of Molasses 151

Hen-NEIGH the Hoover! 153

I Wonder If I'm Missing Something Obvious? 155

You've Sneezed Your Last 156

Should We Tell Him? 158

Is it a Bird? Is it a Plane? NO! It's a Monk! 160

Swanning Around Like They Own the Place 162

Who Turned Out The Lights?! 164

Ghost Ships Are a Thing of the Past! Right? 166

It's Your Job to Wash the Loincloths, Son..168

Okay, Who Ordered the Banana Supreme with Extra Banana
and Banana Fries? 170

"Bless You! Bless You! Bless You! Now Please Shut Up" 172

Dear Me, I Am Pleased That I Have Responded To Me... 173

Honor Even in War 175

I Have This Voice in my Head That Just Won't Leave..........................177

La Mancha Negra 179

I Thought We Were Friends! 181

Everyone Has a Little Bit of Bart Simpson Deep Down........................183

Pineapple Insurance Might be Sensible at That Price............................185

The Rhythm is Gonna Getcha! Getcha into the Grave! 186

Watching Clowns Only Lands You in Trouble, or the River 188

It's a Condition called *IMANALCOHOLICITIS* 190

Sometimes, Cheaters Do Prosper 96

Do We Think He's Dead Yet? 98

Double the Diapers and Double the Crying 100

Three Lives Down, Six Left 101

The Unluckiest Luckiest Man Ever 103

Hemingway's New Atlantis 105

"1st Place To Mrs. Miggins For Screaming At Bob!" 107

I Think They Bought It… 109

Castro and the Painted Seashell 111

They Shall Not Growl Old 113

Teletubbies Say GO AWAY! 115

I'd Take it Over Telemarketing 116

Seriously, What is the Big Deal About it? 118

The Competitively Bearded Drug Dealer 120

This Bite Might Be Your Last 121

Kebab, Anyone? 123

"You're Under Arrest for Possession of a Ghastly Hat" 125

Listerine Or Listurine? 127

The Toxic Lady 129

General Sedgwick's Famous Last Words 130

You Picked the Wrong House! Now Sit Down and Eat 132

You'll Have to Come in, I'm on the Lavatory 134

Turkeys: The OG Bald Eagle 136

Which One of You Taught Him to Say That? 137

Inky the Escape Artist 139

The Great U-Bend That Fought the Nazis 140

That'll Show Those Pesky Editors 142

INTRODUCTION

Our lives are made up of tens of thousands of stories. The big stories, decades-long, that tell of your meteoric rise from Graphic Designer all the way to the heights of Senior Graphic Designer. The tiny stories, mere seconds in length, document your failure to peel a potato without managing to shave off your fingerprint. All of these stories are important in some way to someone: many are lost, many more are forgotten and a select few may forever be brought up by your friends in front of that cute person you've been trying to chat up at a late-night bar.

Some estimates (or at least, a quick Google) say that there are and have been 117 billion humans on Earth over recorded time. Allow a moment to ponder this. 117 billion. That means that those 117 billion people have very likely had lives of some sort with something happening in them that's worth telling - so why don't we hear a select few?

We must be selective, of course. We can't just find any old story to tell. Who'd want to hear about how many times Stanley Toltoton from Derby, UK goes to the pub each year? Even Stanley doesn't want to. The fact is that although there are thousands upon thousands of stories in each person's life, many are very dull. When stories aren't dull, they can be upsetting or grief-laden, like someone becoming sick or dying, and no one wants to construct a book that makes you unhappy. At the same time, there are joyful events that we experience, such as realizing you didn't, in fact, burn the Quesadilla you were making, or that you've re-found your sunglasses. Yet, basically, joy doesn't make for great reading either. It's often best left for those experiencing it, to have it in the moment. Like a plate of nachos.

This book is not about dull stories or those tiny moments of joy. No, this book is filled with hysterical anecdotes that took place from prehistorical civilizations up to the present. From how Egyptians could tell a woman was pregnant to the story of America's first and only

1

emperor, these short and hilarious tales are bound to bring out a chuckle in even the most stoic of crowds.

This book will provide you with exceptional knowledge. You'll learn incredible things! Monumental information that the great brains of history could only wish for! Or, at the very least, you'll learn some nuggets of info that might help you on a quiz night. But most of all, you're going to have a laugh, chuckle, giggle, or you'll suppress your laughter so much that you do an embarrassing little snort on the train, and everyone will look at you. This compilation of food history, witty war blunders, brave animals, and the worst political faux pas will have co-workers and friends rolling with laughter.

Every story written on these pages is true, mostly. Feel free to skip through the book as you wish, find a title that intrigues you from the contents, and read on. In the words of Lord Byron: "Always laugh when you can. It is a cheap medicine."

GUERRILLA WARFARE AGAINST FLIGHTLESS BIRDS

Typically, the word "war" evokes images of soldiers and guns, not wildlife. But, in 1932 the Australian army went to war with emus, flightless birds that resemble ostriches, in what has become known as the *Great Emu War*. This is not the funniest part of the story: not only did the Australian army wage war on birds, but they also lost.

So, why did the Australian government declare war on birds?

Emus are native to Australia, but in the 1930s they were wreaking havoc on the local farmland. Every year emus migrate from the coast inland so they can reproduce. At the time of the Emu War, 20,000 emus made the first aggressive move by deciding that farmland in Campion was the best place for them to breed. They destroyed farmers' wheat crops and damaged fences, which then resulted in rabbits launching their own small invasion and causing further crop damage.

Farmers in the region already had it tough with wheat prices plummeting and the Australian government withholding the promised subsidies to farmers. A group of ex-soldiers from the region went to speak to the Minister of Defense about the emu problem, and it was decided that the military would be sent to the region.

The first battle of the Great Emu War was no laughing matter to the Australian government. Soldiers armed themselves with the top 'Lewis' machine guns and over 10,000 rounds of ammunition. The birds were obviously unarmed, but most of the emus seemed to evade the shooting due to their agility. Some reports claim that they were exceptionally tough and weren't perturbed by the onslaught. Almost all of the emus escaped the first attack. *1-0.*

The Australian media had a field day covering the massive failure and continued to weigh in on war strategies to take down the menacing birds. The government found the whole thing quite funny and joked about providing war medals for the emus.

By the end of November, the Australian military was aggressively hunting emus. Soldiers responded to reports every day of more birds flocking in the area. Many strategies were attempted to counter the attack. Soldiers got close and shot the birds from all directions and cars were driven at the birds, but the casualties remained pitifully low. The army even shifted to guerrilla warfare but to no avail. With every new strategy, the emus adapted to the battle.

The war lasted for a solid 38 days of serious battle. Soldiers swore the emus adopted tactical strategies to counter their attacks and even appointed leaders of their emu packs. In the entire 38-day offensive, only a few hundred emus were killed. After realizing that the entire ordeal had been completely ineffective, the Australian government decided to call off the Emu War on December 10, 1932. Instead of sending the army to battle with the emus, the government decided it was a better idea to arm the farmers with free ammunition, hoping they would take care of the issue. They even put bounties on emus so that farmers would try harder to eradicate them. In the end, the only thing that worked was harvesting the crops. My word, it's almost like that was what was attracting them in the first place…

Today, farmers in Australia still build tall fences to try to keep emus from destroying their crops. The estimated emu population in Australia is now between 600,000 and 700,000.

"I CAN'T GO WHEN WATCHED!"

For those who aren't aware, the men's urinals are a place of quiet and non-discussed etiquette. For instance, if you are the first into the bathroom and are presented with three urinals as such:

1 | 2 | 3

It is customary to take either urinal 1 or 3 in this situation, not to take urinal number 2. Then we are presented with this situation if we consider "Y" to be You.

Y | 2 | 3

The next "customer" walks in and then, if in the right state of mind, will take urinal 3 and everyone will be happy in their lives. Let us allow "T" to be Them.

Y | 2 | T

If you instead take urinal 2 in this scenario, then you've made the whole bathroom experience very awkward, and everyone will loathe you internally. Let us allow "☺" to be you to show off your smug face and stupid way of thinking.

1 | ☺ | 3

Nowadays, we like to be separated when we are doing our business unless we're at a music festival, in which case it seems to be that many don't mind finishing that particular task within splashing distance of each other. However, it hasn't always been this way, public bathrooms have historically been discourteous to personal privacy and there is no better example of this than in Roman public bathrooms.

The Romans are rightfully praised for their pioneering, especially when it came to civil engineering and sanitation. They created the *latrinae*, bathrooms where there exists a single latrine for a single person's use. It was basically a modern-day toilet; the only difference was that most had to be emptied by hand or washed by hand whereas our modern-day toilets flush everything away for us.

The Romans also created something that makes many want to shrivel up into a ball of their own self-consciousness and disappear: the *foricae*. These were essentially public bathrooms, which would often be found next to the public baths. Foricae differs greatly from the latrinae in that it's not one singular unit for one singular person – no, no, no. Instead, there would be one room and one big unit into which everyone would deposit their leavings at the same time. If you imagine a square, the drop-off-points would be placed along every wall of the square facing inward. So, you would be doing your business while looking square into the eyes of your neighbor, local politicians, or even your father-in-law!

Many struggle to talk while on the loo - imagine having to go while staring straight at someone. Never mind the smell!

CARROT SUBTERFUGE

Parents tell their children to eat their carrots because it's good for their eyes and will help them see at night. Lies! While carrots are high in Vitamin A, therefore making them good for eyesight, carrots are no more likely than a cheeseburger to make people see in the dark.

It seems likely that a group of parents banded together to spread this barrel of untruths to entice children to eat their vegetables. Yet this myth actually stems from a ruse worked up by the English during World War II to prevent the Germans from realizing they had developed a top-secret radar technology.

The new technology was called Airborne Interception Radar (AI), and it had the ability to locate German bombers before they even got to the English Channel.

The first pilot to shoot down an enemy plane utilizing this new technology was military civil aircraft pilot John Cunningham, who became known as "Cat Eyes Cunningham," because of his extensive number of nighttime kills. When the press picked up on old Cat Eyes, the British Ministry of Information began telling them that the reason for his nighttime victories was that the pilot ate an abundance of carrots.

Whether or not the Germans believed the myth is unclear; however, British citizens certainly bought into the war-time propaganda. During this time the British government frequently issued blackouts to make it more difficult for the German planes to hit their targets, so any suggestion of something that could help people see at night was an easy sell. Ads started popping up containing messages like, "Carrots keep you healthy and help you see during the blackout."

Following these ads, Britain became carrot-crazed. In part of their call to get citizens to grow victory gardens to win the war on the "food front," they implemented a cartoon character called "Dr. Carrot," a terrifying cartoon of a carrot with a dimpled chin and hairy carrot strings for eyebrows.

The campaign for Dr. Carrot went so far that even Disney played a part. A Disney cartoonist created a whole carrot family - Carroty George, Pop Carrot, and Clara Carrot - which the British used in their ads to the public.

Most likely the British were less concerned about the public eating their vegetables and more concerned about the lack of sugar rations, and their 100,000-ton surplus of carrots. This contributed to the reasoning behind their marketing of disgusting recipes like carrot pudding, with carrots being the key ingredient used to replace sugar.

Anyone interested in this popular myth can learn more about it at the World Carrot Museum, the first virtual museum in the world, and the only museum dedicated to teaching the world about carrots.

BIZARRE FOOD ORIGINS

Did you ever think about a common food or product that was originally named something else? It's more common than one would think to name something terrible off the bat and rebrand it later to appeal to consumers' tastes (and taste buds.)

Kiwifruit, the common green fruit with little black seeds, was originally named Chinese gooseberries. As its original name suggests, kiwifruit, originated in China. Monkeys loved kiwifruit, and before it was the Chinese gooseberry, it was named "mihoutao," which translates to macaque fruit. Apparently, monkeys were big fans of the kiwi and that's where the first name came from.

Chinese gooseberry seeds were brought to New Zealand from China in 1904 by Mary Isabel Fraser. Ms. Fraser was the principal of an all-girls school in New Zealand and was traveling with her sister, Katie Fraser, to visit mission schools. The women ended up in Ichang, China and it was here Mary got her hands on the seeds that would ultimately become the kiwifruit.

Ms. Fraser gave the seeds to a farmer, Alexander Allison, who turned out to have a green thumb. He planted the seeds and in 1910 the vines began to bear delicious kiwifruit. After people began trying the fruit, they named it the Chinese gooseberry because the flavor resembled that of a gooseberry.

The timing of the sale of kiwifruit to the United States during the Cold War became problematic. A fruit named "Chinese" anything was not going to sell.

Turners and Growers first decided to change the name to "melonette" but that was ultimately unsuccessful. It comes as no surprise that one didn't work. A kiwi tastes absolutely nothing like a melon! They then decided to choose the name kiwifruit in June 1959.

It turns out that kiwi is not the only food that started off with a different name. Candy corn used to be called "chicken feed," Eggo waffles were originally called "froffles," and cotton candy was originally known as "fairy floss." The iconic McDonald's Big Mac was originally named the "Aristocrat or Blue Ribbon Burger" and was wildly unpopular until they rebranded it, while Kool-Aid was first branded as Fruit Smack and came in glass bottles that were continuously breaking.

THE PAINS AND STRUGGLES OF WINNING THE LOTTERY

Nothing ever happens in an Alabama Waffle House, not even when you win the lottery there on a Sunday morning. It is always business as usual, and usually, business is slow. Truckers driving north all look alike after 10 straight hours of driving, and every tourist heading to Disneyworld wears the same clothes. Not many of either group stop at the restaurant, and those who do are usually after the bathroom. Urgently. Even the regulars are few and far between, but they are, well, regular.

Ed Skewer was one of them. He would come in early every Sunday for breakfast and order his French toast with extra hashbrowns. With a big round belly, pants an inch lower than they should be, and a mustache for the ages, Ed was a regular in every way. Since he was also known for tipping in lottery tickets, most of the waitresses preferred to pass his table along. It's not like they were going to win anything. And poor Ed didn't really have the funds to tip on a French toast breakfast at the Waffle House.

Tonda, Ed's favorite waitress, didn't bother writing down the tip amount on his receipts any longer. They both followed the same routine every Sunday. Ed would arrive at 6:30, ask for a coffee, and read the local news. "Two sugars, one cream. Please." He would then order at seven, be done eating half an hour later, tip Tonda one lottery ticket, and head out the door at a quarter to eight. Nobody knew what Ed did, or where he went, except on Sunday mornings.

It was only later that week when Tonda realized she had a winning ticket. The lady on the TV told her so. "Ten million dollars," she said. Enough to leave Alabama and find a sweet home somewhere else. The following Sunday morning, she quietly told Ed about it and asked him to keep it to himself. "Sure, sweetheart," he said. Tonda believed him right up until he told the other waitresses and sued her for the cost of a brand-new truck. The waitresses sued her too, wanting to split the winnings. Then the manager. And her ex-husband. Even the IRS took her to court, asking for more taxes, of course. The usual.

And it is always the usual at the Waffle House, even if you win the lottery there. It's the days after that you need to worry about. After surviving those, Tonda left town in search of a safer job and better tips and found both as a poker dealer at a Las Vegas casino.

THE SILENT CRIMINAL

A few criminals are masterminds of their craft and conspire to secretly steal billions of dollars behind our backs. Most of them end up in politics. Other outlaws prefer a more hands-on approach to crime, like robbing banks and gas stations. Some of them are pros, some are not. Then there are the odd lawbreakers who challenge our core beliefs regarding what constitutes a crime, and how to punish it. They come about only so often and are often more absurd than dangerous. Silent man is one of them.

Nobody knows where he comes from. He won't say. His crime and punishment? Standing in the middle of a busy road, is punishable by one month in county jail. Upon his release, Silent man would always go back to the same intersection, and stand in the same road. He would go to jail again, then rinse and repeat. Locals gossiped about where he came from, but nobody knew his name, not even his own lawyer. He refused to talk to the court-appointed doctor too, so it was impossible to determine if he was sane or not.

His fingerprints were in the system, and following every arrest a positive match is made, but there was only an alias. Silent man. Authorities couldn't keep him locked up. "It is unconstitutional," his lawyer would say. They never had any idea on what to do with him, or how to keep him from his mischievous ways. At first, cars would honk at him, but they soon realized the futility of it and opted for driving around him instead. Teens loved to dress up as him on Halloween and stand in the middle of the road until the police arrived.

Not surprisingly, it was during every late October that speculation reached a boiling point. Cheap local news outlets and tabloids had several theories on who he was, and what he wanted. *The Daily Mail* claimed Silent man was a "harbinger of the apocalypse." *The Daily Bogus* produced several pages of questionable evidence contending that he was JFK's real killer. When Silent man's lawyer forced them to retract, they published a new, even more scandalous headline: "Nasa files unsealed! Silent man's identity revealed!" The article went on to describe him as a stranded extraterrestrial suffering from memory loss. And a virgin.

Whether Silent man can speak but chooses not to or is actually mute remains up for debate. A general point of agreement, on the other hand, is how much nicer it would be to hear more about guys like him instead of the usual politicians.

HOW DO THEY CATCH IT?

Have you ever eaten haggis before? If not, then the Scottish dish comes highly recommended, so long as you don't mind eating something that is, in principle, quite disgusting.

Haggis is a mixture of offal, oatmeal, suet, onion, and spices encased in the lining of sheep's stomach, and it's surprisingly quite delicious. However, the Scottish have played a brilliant prank about haggis almost universally as a culture for decades. A poll in 2003 found that one-third of US visitors to Scotland believed in the prank. The legend is of the Wild Haggis.

The Scottish have peddled a legend of an animal that is called the haggis and is, of course, where haggis *actually* comes from. Of course, you can have the manufactured fake haggis, but everyone knows that you have to catch a real one to know its true taste. The legend of the wild haggis says that its left and right legs are different lengths, which means that it theoretically can run in circles easily. So, this makes them difficult to hunt because they can sprint up thin hills and mountains with surprising dexterity. Thus, steep hillsides and mountains are its home.

There are supposedly different types, too: some haggis' (or haggi) have shorter left legs than right legs as mentioned or the same can be true in reverse. This means that some types of haggis are better suited to running clockwise and some are well-versed in running counter-clockwise. They get along perfectly well but can't breed because the male needs to turn its body to face the same way as the female, and when he does thus, he loses his balance and topples over.

If anyone asks you if you want to go on a Haggis Hunt, wink, tap your nose and say, "I won't, but that American chap over there just might."

A SWORD ATOP THE MOUNTAIN

By 1907, Mount Tsurugi was the only mountain left unclimbed in the Japanese Archipelago. Every local mountaineer dreamed of being first to the top. There were fights at bars on the weekends whenever a drunk climber claimed to have been there. Some men came close to death during their ascents. Others spent every waking minute preparing for the climb, like Yoshitaro Shibasaki.

Yoshitaro woke up every morning at four to meditate and do his breathing exercises. He ate a light breakfast before going for a quick run and then spent the later afternoon hiking in the nearby mountains. If there had ever been a man who could conquer Mount Tsurugi, Yoshitaro was it. After years of preparation, he finally secured financing from a local noblewoman and traveled to the base of the mountain looking for immortality.

It was an arduous climb. One of his men had to return after the second day. Another one stayed behind on the expedition's final approach to the summit. Of the eight to make it, half fell ill upon reaching their goal, and the rest couldn't shake the feeling that they were not alone. Unshaken, Yoshitaro delivered a passionate speech he had prepared beforehand. Or at least most of it, until one of his men pointed to a pile of rocks and spoke out of turn. A rough translation of the original Japanese, recorded in the expedition's journal, is something along the lines of "Hey guys, is that a sword sticking out over there?"

To everyone's surprise, it was! It looked ancient and had a curved, ornamental handle and a straight blade rusted to black. Yoshitaro was devastated. Someone had been there before him! Upon his return, he offered the sword to his generous patron and went on to climb many other mountains over the years, some of them higher than Tsurugi. But he could never shake the feeling that someone had beaten him to the top.

Decades after Yoshitaro's death, a thorough scientific analysis revealed the sword to be over 1,000 years old and to have belonged to an ancient warrior from the Nara period. And just as scientists had worked hard in dating the sword, a group of paranormal researchers claimed the warrior himself had contacted them while camping near the mountain. He had told them to please point him toward the local museum. Apparently, he had forgotten his sword at the top and needed it before moving on to the afterlife.

A NICE NAZI
IS STILL A NAZI

If I were to ask you who the worst people of all time were, you'd give a couple of answers: Al-Qaeda, the British Empire, Stalin, and inevitably, the Nazis. The Nazis were a fascistic, antisemitic political party that ruled Germany throughout the 1930s and are responsible for World War II and the deaths of tens of millions of people. Without a doubt, awful people, who did awful things.

There is a name, however, that may cause historians to give a wry smile, particularly if they've had a few drinks. That name is Hanns Scharff.

Now Hanns Scharff was a member of the Luftwaffe and was their chief interrogator. When a prisoner of war was captured, it was his job to extract information from them through any means necessary. He had carte blanche to do whatever it took: pull out their fingernails, beat them up, or even play them George Formby's back catalog. Hans Scharff didn't do any of this.

Instead, Hans would take the prisoner on a nice walk with no guards present. He might sit them down and have a few beers, perhaps bring them some bread that he'd baked at home. He'd basically be friendly. Invariably, Scharff was able to extract valuable information from highly trained soldiers who were probably receiving the best treatment that they could from any soldier on the planet.

One prisoner, the master fighter pilot Lt. Col. Francis Gabreski, was proud to hold the title as one of the very few prisoners who never gave information over to Scharff. Upon meeting Gabreski, Scharff had greeted him with delight; he admired Gabreski's flying and had hung his picture in his office for months before he met him. They enjoyed their time together and after the war remained firm friends, even going so far as to re-enact the "interrogation" in 1983 at a reunion event.

Hanns Scharff was so well respected that at the end of World War II, he was permitted to migrate to America. After testifying against an American pilot who had defected to Nazi Germany, he became one of the 20th century's leading mosaic artisans. His work can be seen to this day in the California State Capitol building, Los Angeles City Hall and the Epcot Center at Disney World in Florida. It depicts the story of *Cinderella*. I wonder how many people who go and look at the expertly crafted mosaic know that the creator was once the best interrogator of prisoners in Nazi Germany.

THE HABITS OF NIKOLA TESLA, NIKOLA TESLA, NIKOLA TESLA

Nikola Tesla. One of the great pioneers and inventors. Tesla is not just the name of a car that runs out of charge halfway across your city, Tesla is the man who developed practical uses for alternating current electricity. He invented many things that helped pave the way for humankind's mastery of electricity, such as better lights, transformers, oscillators, and the wonders of vegetarianism.

However, like many who are blessed with intelligence or a pioneering spirit, Tesla lived a tortured life. He used to have visions of blinding light, some say an inspiration for his work, and he had OCD, Obsessive Compulsive Disorder. OCD is often characterized nowadays by a desire to have order and cleanliness in one's home. Often people say, "sorry, it's my OCD!" as they put a plate in the dishwasher. Or some say, "I'm a bit OCD about this," when they turn a light switch off (something that I think flies in the face of both Tesla and OCD sufferers).

OCD is serious for those who are truly afflicted with it, but it can result in some humorous and varied behavior patterns. Tesla, for instance, was compelled to do things in threes, which led him to only occupy hotel rooms that were divisible by three, as well as walk around a building three times before he'd enter it. He also despised shiny jewels, essentially fearing them; he couldn't stand to be around pearl or diamond earrings. He constantly washed his hands for fear of germs and as he ate or drank, he'd calculate the cubic particles of soup, coffee, or food.

People are often obsessed with Elon Musk, the owner of Tesla, and his routines and habits. Perhaps we should instead be focusing on the original Tesla's habits instead - at least then we'd all maybe get closer to our 10,000 steps a day.

"HEY ALEXA! BUTT OUT OF MY RELATIONSHIP!"

Ah, Alexa, Siri, and Google. The main trifecta of helpful automated assistants that come attached to our smartphones or speakers that litter our homes. We call out all sorts of instructions to them, feeling like Meryl Streep in *The Devil Wears Prada*, for the AI to diligently listen and carry out our every whim.

"Hey, Alexa! Add Midsummer Night's Dream *to my shopping basket."*

"Okay. Ordering 70 mattresses to the home address."

How useful they can be. The vision that anyone has with these kilobyte PAs is futuristic, *Iron Man*-esque in fact, but many people have taken to venting their frustrations online about the repeated failures with their devices. Here are a select few problems or stories that real customers have reported, tweeted, and commented about:

"One of my supervisor's kids was telling her a joke in front of her Alexa. Out of nowhere, Alexa said, 'That's a funny joke' and then proceeded to tell her own joke." No one likes 'one-uppers' Alexa, come on.

"Out of the blue, late one night, after I hadn't talked to Alexa for hours, Alexa said, 'If Chuck Norris wants you to know where he is, he'll find you. If he doesn't, you won't know until it's too late.' I wasn't aware that Alexa was being programmed to engage using memes from 2009, but there we go.

"My wife and I were arguing about something, and things were getting a little heated. I don't know what my Alexa heard, but she suddenly interjected with, 'Why don't we change the subject?' It was unexpected and relevant enough to be creepy and we still talk about it some years later." Alexa's braver than most! Have you ever tried to stop a couple arguing before? I'm just amazed they listened.

"I moved my Echo Dot to the bathroom so I could listen to music in the shower, but the first time I went to pee in the night with it in there, I heard the

little "ding" and saw the blue light that shows she was listening. Unplugged immediately." What on earth is Bezos doing? I can't even go to the bathroom without being monitored now!

"The other night, out of the blue, Alexa started making a crazy scary ghostly wail, like a child crying, for about four seconds. Wtf???" It seems too obvious, but this sounds like a follow-up to *The Ring*. Perhaps we can do *The Ring II: Alexa's Revenge* and the ring is the blue ring on the speaker? Quick, Alexa! Get me Warner Bros on the phone!

Hopefully, your Alexa behaves itself and does as it's told; just keep an eye on your Amazon basket. I don't remember adding 19 Amazon Echos…, I think she's amassing an army.

WATCH OUT! THAT'S THE EMANCIPATOR'S MUSIC!

When we think about American presidents, there are many recognizable faces among the 46 leaders who have, for the most part, dominated global politics. JFK, George Bush, Barack Obama, Donald Trump, Ronald Reagan, and so on and so forth, the US presidents are the most famous politicians in the Western world, if we don't count Scrooge McDuck. The most recognizable of all, however, is probably Abraham Lincoln. With his steely gaze, large chin, and tall hat, he is unmistakable by anyone…, apart from a silhouette of Jack the Ripper.

Lincoln is best known for his Proclamation Emancipation in which he renounced slavery and declared it illegal in the United States of America, bringing a formal end to a centuries-long practice. He is also known as a martyr for the Union of America following his infamous assassination in 1865 at the end of the American Civil War at the hands of John Wilkes Booth. If the cinema is anything to go by (which it's not), we're also led to believe he was a vampire hunter, though this may have been exaggerated in the 2012 film. What many aren't aware of, however, is that Abraham Lincoln holds a spot in the Wrestling Hall of Fame with an almost impeccable record, facing defeat only once in his entire career.

That's right! Before Lincoln became a national hero as a politician and leader, he was grappling with opponents! Performing daredevil backflips and clotheslines and developing his signature move, **THE EMANCIPATION.** That last sentence isn't quite true, but while he was a champion wrestler, it's just more fun to imagine him as a modern-day WWE muscle-man stuffed into a black leotard.

Lincoln was a county-wrestling champion by the age of 21, and it is no huge surprise since he stood at 1.95m and was a well-built, naturally strong man. The story goes that he once fended off a group of bullies in New Salem, Illinois in a contest with their leader Jack Armstrong who

23

refused to abide by the rules of traditional wrestling. Despite the underhand tactics employed by Armstrong, he admitted that Lincoln was the better fighter and conceded defeat, bringing Lincoln much admiration from those who heard about the fight.

He was defeated only once in his whole career, at the hands of Hank Thompson during the Black Hawk War of 1832, in which Lincoln was serving. Thompson was himself a soldier and Lincoln congratulated him after he was bested. His wrestling career became public knowledge during his election campaign in 1858 and only helped to cement his reputation as a capable politician. Strength, physical or otherwise, was seen as a necessary quality for a politician. Well, that and absolutely banging entrance music.

ARE YOU GOING
TO EAT WITH THAT?

Teeth are a sensitive topic for many people, either because they're scared of the dentist, or the dentist has become scared of them. We're encouraged to have a perfect smile in the modern world and from Hollywood to models on posters, we see perfect teeth everywhere we look. The aesthetic look behind teeth is a modern obsession. If you'd seen King Henry VIII's teeth, for example, you'd have wondered how he managed to secure one wife, let alone six. But we do need our teeth, for forming words, expressions, and eating - it's pretty crucial for our way of life.

So, what do we do if we lose them? Nowadays we have very accurate, perfect sets of false teeth or dentures that function and look great. They're made from..., magic, probably, but it wasn't always like this. You don't have to go back too far to see dentures that were essentially crafted from wood and if we examine the 19th century, then we'll find something a little more horrifying.

By the 18th century, Europe had a full-blown sugar addiction. Sugar had begun to find its way into common foods and drinks in the continent and Europeans were addicted. Today we are aware of sugar addiction and so companies put it in almost every type of processed food that you can find. It tastes good and is guaranteed to keep the customer coming back for more. The other side of the coin in the 21st century is that we know that sugar causes tooth decay, so we brush our teeth and visit dentists to keep our smiles looking lovely and not like a mouthful of week-old cigarette butts.

In the 1800s, the technology and knowledge weren't there to fight against tooth decay, gum disease was rife, and it was very rare for anyone to reach 50 with their natural teeth. So, there was a desperate need for false teeth. Luckily, there was an abundance of *extra* teeth that weren't being used anymore.

As well as there being a lot of sugar during the 18th and 19th centuries, there was also a lot of war. Thousands and thousands of young men were dying in battlefields across Europe and luckily many of them had mouthfuls of lovely young teeth that could be carefully removed, polished up a bit, and serve as perfectly decent dentures. Even if you couldn't eat with them. After the Battle of Waterloo in 1815, where 50,000 men had died, it became fashionable in England to sport "Waterloo Teeth," supposedly taken from the battlefield (though it's basically impossible to prove that they were or weren't from Waterloo). It wasn't until the 1870s that human teeth stopped being used as dentures and suitable replacements were found…, or at least, that's what they *want* you to think. I suddenly have an urge to floss.

HONEY COME CLOSER, THE FLIES ARE HUNGRY

Honey is a delicious and wonderful product. It's produced by bees, which means that so long as there *are* bees, it is a sustainable good that tastes wonderful in baking, porridge, or even on toast. Given the rising cost of honey in the 21st century, most people are quite sparing with it, but in Ancient Egypt honey was practically thrown around! Literally, it was thrown all over the Pharaoh's favorite slaves. This wasn't as a sort of perfume, or because it made the people shine in a way that the Pharaohs liked.

Instead, the slaves would be coated in honey to attract flies. Pepi II Neferkare was a Pharaoh particularly known for doing this to his slaves. Neferkare took the coveted throne in 2278 BCE at the age of six, and he was contemptuous of the irritating buzzing fly. Many Egyptians had respect for flies, as they were regarded as a symbol of perseverance (and presumably, for their inability to re-discover the window through which they first entered one's living room). Necklaces have been discovered from the period with golden fly amulets dangling from them, thought to have been given to soldiers who fought well in battle.

Neferkare, however, hated the fly, despite its positive attributes and he loathed to be bothered by them. Often cited as having one of the longest rules of all time (sometimes reported as 94 years but more likely to be 64 years), he was known as a bit of an eccentric, which may explain his decision.

So, next time your job feels a bit pointless or tedious, remember that at least you're not having honey smeared all over you so some dude doesn't have to deal with a fly problem.

THAT WOULD HURT
A CHOCO-LOT!

If someone were to assassinate you, how do you think they'd do it? If they were any self-respecting, professional assassin then they'd find a pattern in your daily routine and use that to their advantage. Do you walk the same way to work every day? Do you hang out at the same place on the weekends? Or maybe you like a particular snack, that you indulge in regularly.

This was the reality facing Winston Churchill, the British Prime Minister during World War II who was in charge of managing England in the long conflict against Nazi Germany. His job brought a massive amount of pressure with it, which may have explained some of his less healthy habits. Churchill's routine was well publicized in the decades after his death. Supposedly, Churchill would rise at 7:30 a.m. every day with, one imagines, a huge hangover. For the next three and a half hours, he worked in bed and ate a monumental breakfast before rising at 11 a.m., whereby he'd have a whisky and soda with a small walk. At 1 p.m. he'd drink heavily with a quite colossal lunch and smoke cigars before returning to work near 3:30 p.m...., or he'd play games. At about 5 p.m. he'd disappear for a small nap, presumably because the words "TOP SECRET" had started to read as "TROOP CIRCUIT," and then rose at 6:30 p.m. for dinner at 8 p.m. Dinner went on well past midnight with much cigar-smoking, brandy-drinking, and - in all likelihood - some planning of how to win the war. He then went to bed in the early hours of the morning.

What is clear is that we're all jealous of Winston Churchill. BUT his lifestyle was predictable. The man enjoyed drinking and eating to excess, which the Nazis were aware of. They sought to take out Churchill through a variety of methods but largely through disguising highly deadly and explosive traps as food items bound for the PM's office.

During the war, MI5 (the British intelligence agency) uncovered several plots aimed at Ol' Winnie C. Explosive devices were made to look like shaving brushes, cans of fruit, lumps of coal, and bangers and mash with an extra bang but none ever made it to the vicinity of the esteemed politician. The closest they got to completing their fiendishly clever plot was by creating an innocent-looking chocolate bar that was actually a fast-acting explosive that activated if you cracked a block of the bar off. Churchill was a known lover of the confectionary and if the bar had made its way into his office, or even his bed chamber, he'd likely have struggled to resist!

MI5 spotted the bar for what it was, and it never made it that far. But it's yet another notable bizarre assassination attempt story - so bizarre that it almost worked.

YOU'RE NOT LEAVING THIS TABLE UNTIL YOU'RE SEEING DOUBLE!

Medieval England is rarely known as a time of enlightenment, good fortune, or great ideas. The average person could barely write their own name, wealth was reserved for only the top 1%, and one-third of children didn't live past the age of five. For hundreds of years, many in society were left to work excruciatingly hard every day of the week so they could be rewarded with some of life's basics. Thank God we've moved on..., amen.

It wasn't *all* doom and gloom, however. The ever-gleaming promise of a paradise-like afterlife kept many happy during their lives, communities banded together at times of celebration, and the people drank beer like they breathed the air. Children in their late infancy and teenage years partook in beer drinking regularly too; in fact, many in English society would start their day by drinking and wouldn't really stop until their heads hit the pillow at night. Thank God we've moved on..., amen.

But why? Why did they drink so much? Some records tell us that many civilians would generally choose beer over water, given the choice, so it could simply have been a preference thing. After all, health was not high on the agenda in the 14th century. If you complained of sickness, you may have a chicken strapped to you if you're lucky or all the blood would be drained out of you if you were very unlucky. People didn't really know that daily and constant alcohol consumption is incredibly bad for you in the long run, mainly because their run was normally rather short. If you did die from alcohol-induced liver failure, no one would know. It would probably be put down to the Devil's work or God's work, depending on your outlook on life.

To be fair, the beer consumed in Medieval England was called 'small beer' and the ABV sat at 2.8%, which is almost half as strong as a regular beer in modern-day England, or twice as strong as the average

American beer. The upshot of this was that society functioned. The landscape wasn't filled with tottering, staggering peasants falling onto their pitchforks, as at 2.8%, ABV with manual labor and food is unlikely to have much of an effect. Most wouldn't "get drunk," so to speak.

Some historians have claimed that beer was safer to drink than water and so most *chose* the beer out of courtesy for their own health! Try that one out next time you're at work:

"What this? Well, actually, I've heard that water's full of impurities and artificial vitamins nowadays, so I'm instead going to sip away at this delicious glass of Indian Pale Ale. I'll let you know when there are two computer monitors instead of one."

There may be some merit in this but in Medieval England, most villages were built around a water source such as a stream or river, which provided a near-constant source of fresh and safe water. The idea of it being safer is largely a myth; most people can instinctively tell when a drink isn't right and if you taste stale or uns~~...~~ter, you sure know about it.

No, it was actually a fuel thing. Beer was simple and provided a boost to the start of your day, fueling you up for your grueling work. Try it one day and get back to us. As long as you don't have an addictive personality.

NO ONE'S TAKING
THAT RECORD FROM HER

Many people have a fear of flying. The most common reasons for that fear are – fear of being out of control, fear of the unknown, fear of heights, claustrophobia, and fear of the plane crashing. All are totally legitimate. Flying isn't a natural thing for people to do, and there is an inherent danger in long-distance travel, but you're still far safer in a plane than you are if you end up on the wrong end of a donkey.

For Vesna Vulovic, a Serbian air stewardess, a few of these fears came together in an unbelievable story on 26 January 1972.

Vulovic was working on board a Yugoslav Airlines flight on an otherwise normal day when an explosion pulsed through the aircraft. She wasn't initially supposed to work on that flight, but a scheduling error left her to do the shift. It was suspected to be a briefcase bomb, a deliberate attempt to destroy the plane and endanger the 28 passengers and crew. The bomb detonated over Czechoslovakia and the plane erupted into debris, cascading through the air alongside 28 bodies.

Vulovic was the only one still alive as she began a Guinness World Record-winning free-fall of over 6.2 miles. She was discovered by a woodsman named Bruno Honke who had heard Vulovic screaming in the darkness. He discovered her with her uniform covered in blood. She was in agony. Honke had been a medic during World War II, so used his expertise to keep her alive until the emergency services got there.

The theory is that Vulovic survived by remaining trapped in a food cart inside the destroyed fuselage of the plane. It did a free-fall into some woods with blankets of snow that cushioned the impact somewhat. She still suffered greatly, falling into a coma in hospital and suffering years of paralysis. She regained movement within 10 months of the crash and puts her survival down to her Serbian stubbornness as well as her excessive spinach and chocolate eating as a child.

"I'M MORE OF A GOD GUY"

The role of Pope is one of great responsibility as well as a great privilege. The Pope is the undisputed head of the Catholic Church, which currently has more than a billion followers and has been the Western world's dominant religion for over 1,000 years. Popes are seen as being chosen by God, the closest a human can get to the great almighty without perishing first and so their word is taken rather seriously. If the Pope says something, then it's likely that God told him to say it. This is, of course, how the Pope gets out of paying for their morning Cappuccino.

Not all Popes have acted as one might expect Popes to act, however. They are still fundamentally people and prone to errors, as all leaders are. A few exemplar stories:

- Pope Stephen VI, in the 9th century, dug up the corpse of the previous pope and put it on trial. The body was found guilty of perjury. Stephen was later strangled to death by the supporters of the previous pope.
- Sixtus IV (imagine if he'd been Sixtus VI!) fathered many illegitimate children, which is completely illegal within the Catholic Church. What's worse is that one of them was fathered with his own sister! He did go on, however, to commission the Sistine Chapel.... Sis-tine. Sis.... We can read too much into names, can't we?
- In 1513, Leo X officially allowed people to buy their way into heaven via a gift of money to the church known as an "indulgence," a practice that was decried by many Christians and actually led to the Christian church splintering into different sects.

A bizarre story that tickles the funny bone especially (and has led the writer of this book to spend days wondering if there's a good God/Dog pun that can be written down) is the story of Pope Gregory IX who in 1233 announced a war on cats.

Gregory saw cats as Satan in a fur coat and had been suspicious of them for decades before he became pope. Perhaps the fact that cats were so domesticated and *everywhere* played into it, but it was largely due to forced confessions about the nature of satanic interactions from lowly peasants across Europe gathered by the church. 1233, the year of the *Catastrophe* (it's not actually called this) rolled around and thousands upon thousands of cats were mercilessly slaughtered. It was thought that the devil then spread the plague as punishment for his fallen slaves, but actually it was simply that after killing the cats, nothing was available to kill the rats that housed the fleas that spread the plague.

As you can probably tell, not all the cats were killed, and we think they are still just as 'pawsome' as ever.

"HE'S NOT THE MOST SOCIAL CHAP"

Many of us value some time alone, especially after a busy week of work or socializing. A moment to not be bothered, read a book, watch a movie, sit and watch nature, or perhaps do nothing at all. Modern-day introverts will refuse social gatherings to spend time with themselves and may even make up outrageous lies or do silly things to make that happen:

> "I'm sorry, I have a doctor's appointment for my uncle's dog's sister, I must attend. Plus, I'm going on a solo barge trip for the next week, so I am totally unavailable for the work drinks and pizza night."

But have you ever committed yourself to total isolation for 37 years because you were bored of people asking you questions? That's what Simeon Stylites decided he'd do in the 5th century CE.

Simeon was a Syrian Christian. From a young age, he showed total and complete devotion to Christianity and entered a monastery at 16 years of age. He was willing to put himself through such hardship and extreme austerity that the monastery decided his behavior couldn't continue in their name so asked him to leave. He went on to spend a year and a half shut in a small hut in relative isolation, even managing to neither eat nor drink anything during Lent. His survival saw the term *miracle* applied to his actions for the first time.

After the hut, Simeon sought better isolation and further tests of his dedication, so he disappeared to a small living space, no more than 22 yards in diameter on the slopes of the Sheik Barakt Mountain (interestingly enough, a similar space in New York City is advertised for $4,000 per month and boasts "scenic viewing" and a "rustic aesthetic").

Pilgrims constantly journeyed to Simeon to ask questions of the man, and he became frustrated with the never-ending attention. He decided that he must become further removed from people so that he could find greater divinity in his life. For that, he needed to be somewhere that he couldn't be found or talked to. He found a 10-foot-tall pillar among some ruins, placed a small platform on top approximately 1.2 square yards and began his stay. He achieved recognition from religious elders who were extremely impressed by his dedication. Simeon only left the pillar to move to a new 50-foot pillar later on.

Simeon received some food over the length of his stay and people kept an eye on him to make sure he was okay. But other than that, he was left alone, as he desired..., well, actually the number of pilgrims visiting him increased rapidly and he would talk to them in the afternoons and presumably thought "What more do I have to do?" He stayed up there for some time between 35 and 42 years and is now seen as a saint for his extreme dedication to the cause.

I'd have avoided being near the pillar shortly after dinner however - when you gotta go, you gotta go.

BUNNIES: FIGHTING BULLIES SINCE 1807

You've probably heard of Napoleon Bonaparte. You may even have seen his face in a portrait. If you're unsure, Napoleon Bonaparte was a fearsome military French leader who ruled from 1799 to 1815. He was ruthless in battle, ruthless in politics, and ruthless when asked how many women named *Ruth* he wanted present at victory celebrations in 1808. He was known around the world as a great threat to European safety; the British especially loathed him, but then again, the British pretty much loathed everyone including themselves for having the bloody nerve to be alive.

In 1807, Napoleon was attending a feast in his honor to celebrate a recent peace treaty with Russia. Several important dignitaries and politicians attended and like all politicians, they were desperate to be near the most powerful person around. The Chief of Staff, Baron Louis-Alexandre Berthier, decided to throw a wonderful Rabbit Hunt after lunch and caught 1,000 little fluffy bunnies to be released into the estate before they would be massacred by several men with guns. Fundamentally, the idea was sound. Napoleon was a keen hunter and soldier, and he fancied himself a superb marksman, so he was delighted to hear that a hunt would be on. There was a great sense of excitement, lunch was quickly finished, and the hunt was announced.

I don't know if you've been around rabbits before, but they're quite nervous. People are scary and rabbits are typically on the wrong end of the food chain to feel like they have the upper hand. The assumption, at this auspicious event, was that the rabbits would take off into the woods, grounds, or nearest mating partner, with some serious speed. The ever-so-brave hunters prepared their weapons, ready to engage in some serious sport to aid the digestion of lunch. Silence fell. A suspense built up and everyone quietened for the event: a few squeaks could be heard, the wind gently blowing through the trees, a pin drop.

RELEASE! The rabbits bolted. Excitement and yelling filled the air. "It's hunting time!" Proclaimed someone, presumably. Napoleon, however, simply paused. Something was wrong, desperately wrong - the rabbits weren't running away at all. In fact, they were running at *him*. The bunnies quickly caught up to Napoleon and scarpered up his jacket, nibbling at his gold buttons, tearing out the stitching, and reducing the resale value by 60%. Napoleon sprinted for his carriage, anything to get him away from the bunnies. They'd become veracious and deadly! Who knows how many men had already been killed? The bunnies galloped (do they gallop?) past him into his carriage and continued their brutal assault inside. As Napoleon was hastily taken into the sunset, away from the disastrous event, the bunnies celebrated in the fields by the estate. They'd succeeded in besting Napoleon in combat, something which few would ever be able to claim.

HEROIN: THE ORIGINAL COUGH MEDICINE

Opium has a history of being some 5,000 years old, its use dating back to 3400 BCE in Asia where the poppy grows naturally. Opium, if you don't know, comes from a certain breed of poppies and can be taken into the human body in various forms. Opium has many effects such as euphoria, relaxation, lower heart rate, and sometimes a small bout of constipation. Opium's modern-day form comes from heroin, which was synthesized in the late 19th century by Felix Hoffmann who worked for the pharmaceutical company *Bayer*. He did this only 11 days after he had synthesized aspirin (what a track record - eh?).

Nowadays, heroin is an illegal drug in most places as it is exceptionally addictive and destructive to people's bodies and lives - however, in the early 20th century, it wasn't viewed in the same way. Bayer saw that heroin was a *very* effective painkiller. Allegedly the name was contrived by the marketing department as a derivative of *heroisch*, meaning heroic and strong. They marketed it as an over-the-counter drug that was more effective and less addictive than morphine and was the best cough suppressant available.

History is full of medical mistakes like this. Doctors were prescribing cigarettes to patients well into the 1960s, soldiers were partaking in methamphetamines during World War II, and many people in 2023 spend six hours a day scrolling through TikTok without concern for their ever-dwindling attention span. The marketing of heroin as a non-addictive cough suppressant, however, was a misstep so severe that it makes these other examples look like a "small whoopsie."

The 1910s were a time of success for Bayer, and they marketed the use of heroin expertly. *Encyclopedia Britannica* wrote glowingly of the product and its various improvements over the use of morphine. The product was sold in many countries and Bayer made lots of money until 1919, after the end of World War I. Unfortunately for the pharmaceutical gods, Germany had lost the war and the winners were rather angry at them. Germany faced massive reparations at the Treaty of Versailles, which included massive amounts of land, money, and possessions being handed over to the Allied powers. This included many of the trademarks that Bayer held, including heroin. Poor Bayer. If only they could have continued, then maybe we'd all be taking heroin and would be much happier…, and dead.

Heroin was outlawed by the League of Nations in the mid-1920s though it had a rising popularity throughout the 20th century and remains a serious problem today. I think I'll stick with Calpol.

PET TU BRUTUS?

The Roman Empire is seen as one of humanity's greatest achievements: the Colosseum, gladiators, art, gods, food, drink and yes, admittedly lots of slavery and war in order to suppress rebellions and subjugate people to the Roman way of life. Regrettably, not all positive. The Romans did, however, feel a very strong affinity with animals and given how large the empire was (12% of the global population), it's no surprise that they began to keep more exotic animals as companions.

Roman worship has been revered in modern times due to the ancient people's ability to see gods as flawed entities with positive and negative traits, rather than being all-seeing, all-knowing, and all-powerful as many modern religions do. Animals were viewed as having affinities or relationships with certain gods and so held particular influence over the Romans. Owls symbolized wisdom due to their association with Athena and dolphins represented rebirth and friendship alongside their relationship with Poseidon.

Though many animals were seen as representations of divine beings, many were simply used for work, like horses, and some were kept because they were pretty or exotic, such as dogs, parrots, or a spoon with a smiley face on it if you were not wealthy.

Ferrets were very common pets in Rome due to their ability to hunt mice, reportedly being far more effective than cats. Monkeys were used for entertainment, which sounds a bit cruel initially until you imagine a monkey butler and suddenly it all makes sense. Famously, lions were used as entertainment as well at Venationes where they would fight skilled gladiators - or serious criminals if some accounts are to be believed. Lions were revered and respected but ultimately arrived at the Colosseum sentenced to death. Elephants were used by the military to strike fear into the hearts of the opposition, as well as the fact that they were about as close to a tank as you can get in 100 CE.

The strangest pets of all were kept by the most powerful, however, the emperors and extremely wealthy. The leaders basically got to have whatever they wanted. Julius Caesar kept a giraffe from Egypt - an oddity he assumed was half camel and half panther! Antonia, daughter of Marc Antony, kept eels and reportedly adored them. Emperor Nero allegedly kept a tigress called Phoebe after he witnessed the fighting spirit it displayed in a Colosseum fight.

The Romans certainly loved their animals more than most people. Keep your eye out for a further extreme example later in this book…

THE FIRST MAN-POWERED ALARM CLOCKS

How do you wake up in the morning? Some people, who live a leisurely life, simply wake up whenever the sunlight touches their face, to the sound of a crested warbler at their window. They rise gracefully from the pillow, stretch for a moment, and sigh as they contemplate how utterly beautiful, they are. They approach their windows and stare out at rolling hills and galloping horses with multi-colored manes. They wander out into their gardens, licking the jellybean flowers and drinking from their chocolate fountains before being given $10,000 by a passer-by for simply being fantastic. Honestly, those people....

But the rest of us? We are graced with responsibility, duties, or an early morning appointment with a doctor -- how do we get up? For most of us, it's an alarm clock or, more likely, an alarm on your phone that pulls you kicking and screaming out of the land of dreams. Alarm clocks are relatively recent inventions. Never mind alarms on your mobile phone, the first adjustable alarm clock wasn't invented until 1847 and that took a few decades to become even remotely affordable for 90% of people.

So, in Victorian English towns and cities, if you needed to be woken up at a certain time for work, you would pay for the services of a Knocker-Up! The Knocker-Ups were highly trained individuals, who possessed something that most could only dream of..., a long stick. The Knocker-Ups were paid a few pence per week to walk around the town or city at the required time in the morning with their aforementioned long stick in hand. They would approach the houses of those who needed waking and, with the slender rod, rap on the household's upper window or door.

They would do this until the person came to the window or door, confirming they were now awake. Legend tells of Percy, the Knocker-

Up who mistakenly knocked on the door of an elderly gentleman on holiday and couldn't stop until he saw the man emerge. He was there for five days before dying from repetitive knocking syndrome. (This may be an exaggerated or entirely fictitious story).

By all accounts, the Knocker-Ups were very reliable and did their job very well. Perhaps Industrial Revolution Britain wouldn't have functioned anywhere near as well if it weren't for the tireless work of the men who made it their mission to wake the workers and businessmen for their days of labor.

However, the real question is: who woke the Knockers-Up up?

LOST IN TRANSLATION

The term "lost in translation" was taken to a whole new level when President Jimmy Carter visited Poland in 1977.

Before he left on his trip, President Carter was assigned an interpreter, like all embarking on a foreign dignitary visit. His interpreter, Steven Seymour, a 31-year-old New Yorker, was chosen by the State Department and was described as the best available Polish interpreter for whom they had security clearances.

On December 29, 1977, upon arriving in Warsaw, President Carter gave a speech that was translated by Steven Seymour.

So, what was lost in the translation? Seymour made not just one but two major errors that have gone down in history. Firstly, Seymour made it sound as if President Carter was abandoning the United States for good. Instead of saying, "I left the United States this morning," Carter's interpreter said, "I left the United States, never to return." Which somewhat caused confusion!

However, he hadn't yet played his winning hand. When President Carter stated that he was happy to be in Poland, the interpreter accidentally said, "he was happy to grasp at Poland's private parts," upsetting many and exciting many more. After the errors were made, the American officials on the trip carried on as if nothing was wrong for a few days and continued to let Seymour interpret for the President in numerous meetings. They simply acted as if nothing out of the ordinary had happened.

Even though the mistakes were made on December 29, Seymour was so unaware of the egregious errors he had made that he didn't even know there was an issue until December 31, when he was approached by an American journalist in the airport requesting comment.

It comes as no surprise that when it came time to make another speech on his trip to Poland, President Carter hired a new interpreter. But again, he was met with disaster. The interpreter struggled to understand the President's English, and fearful of making an inaccuracy, he opted to remain completely silent.

The country of Poland got some great laughs from President Jimmy Carter on that trip, and it's unknown if the interpreter acquired any jobs after.

WHO WON THE
ART-THLETICS THIS YEAR?

The early Olympic games weren't quite what they are now. Technology, awareness around doping, and increasing international attention have made the Olympics an important event for countries the world over every four years. Billions tune in to watch athletes compete in events such as Wrestling, Athletics, Sailing, Weightlifting, Table Tennis, Paint by Numbers, Gymnastics, The L - what? Wait, we DON'T have Paint By Numbers?!

Putting silly jokes aside for a minute, the iterations of sports and events on display at the Olympics change with every four-year cycle, and there have been many sports that have been eradicated since the Olympics started in 1896. To name a few: Tug-of-War, Men's Cross Country, Tandem Cycling, The Rope Climb, Dueling Pistol Shooting, and Art Competitions. Most of these sound like the sort of thing a small village may put on for a "sports day" where tasteless burgers and expensive budget Cola are sold - but they were all legitimate Olympic events for at least two separate Summer Olympics.

The Art Competitions ran from 1912 to 1948 and included many events from the fields of architecture, music, literature, painting, and sculpture that artists could compete in to earn gold, silver, or bronze medals. They didn't have events, unfortunately, for the 100m portrait or perhaps deadlifting Michelangelo's David. The events instead were largely competed in advance, as it were. The stipulations were that the work had to be inspired by sport and couldn't be published before the Olympics.

Germany dominated the table for artistic Olympians with 23 total medals won, while Italy placed a close second with 14. The lowest-ranked country that won any medals was Monaco, which won one less medal than Canada. Bringing artistic competition back brings controversy with it as there are questions over how you award a definite gold in a field that's often seen as being subjective. But maybe things are heading in that direction, as in 2024, Breakdancing will be at the Paris Olympics for the first time. However, it's an equestrian event and must be completed on horseback. (Not true!)

WHEN WILL THE AGE OF THE SILVER FOX BEGIN?

There are several immortal battles that we all engage in and ultimately lose:

1. We battle with Death and must ultimately lose
2. We battle with balancing leisure and work
3. We battle to keep our hair looking even remotely like it did when we were 21.

Now, Battle 1 is unwinnable, so just try not to think about it, and Battle 2 is never-ending. But Battle 3 is potentially winnable if you're willing to lie to yourself just a little. Humans have always been pretty vain and one of the easiest ways to restore a bit of vigor and youth to one's look is to dye your hair. In the 21st century, you have about 4,000 options including bleaching, dying, ombre, highlighting, balayage, or simply using shoe polish (if the guitarist of The Horrors is to be believed). But it wasn't always like this. There was some serious experimentation throughout history to land us at the pinnacle of dyeing.

Famously, the ancient Egyptians dyed their hair. Cleopatra engaged in it herself using henna and lead to hide the grays. The Romans used fermented leeches to turn a head of silver into jet black, although there was little option to dye your hair many other colors until approximately 300 BCE. At this time, sex workers had to have yellow hair to indicate their profession. Some wore wigs, but the right color could be achieved by using ashes from burned plants and nuts. Medieval Europeans strived for blonde hair as fashion moved away from the Roman desire for dark hair. In typical Medieval fashion, there was little too disgusting for them to engage in. One method included mixing honey, white wine, celandine roots, cumin seed, saffron, and box shavings and applying the mixture to your hair for 24 hours before finally washing it all out. It can't have been nice to walk around with that in your hair for 24 hours; you'd be assumed to be both an alcoholic as well as attracting bears from over 50 miles.

It wasn't until the Industrial Revolution that hair dye became more of a formulated and deliberate chemical process after chemist William Henry Perkin accidentally created a dye that turned hair mauve in 1863. Following this, the product (later the company) L'Oréal was founded in 1907, the first commercial hair dye. In the 1960s, hair dye began to move away from necessitating bleach, which can be exceptionally damaging to hair. Today dyeing your hair is commonplace in many societies and spans all sexualities, genders, and cultures.

If one thing's true throughout our thousands of years of society on this planet, it's that we all wish that we didn't have to go gray.

FLY WITH THE ANGELS

Funerals are important to people, but they are undertaken (pun fully intended) in different ways. They might be celebratory with drinks, dancing, food, and a small party as the person's life is toasted, or a sullener affair with readings, poetry, prayer, and tears to mourn the loss of a person that was deeply cared for. Some, however, are just bizarre.

Many people have a small funeral for their pets in one form or another once they've passed - a small burial or cremation is quite common to commemorate the fluffy, feathered, or scaled friend. In Bangkok, Thailand it is popular to pay large sums of money for doggy funerals. One businessman paid the equivalent of $12.5k for a funeral for his pooch that included 60 monks, a procession, and a custom-made gold coffin. Now, for many of us, that's pushing it a bit far, no matter how much we enjoy Fido's woofs, Felix's meows, or the Hamster's..., whatever they do. However, this pales in comparison when we turn our attention back in time to the 1st century BCE.

A quick disclaimer: there is significant debate over whether or not the following story definitely occurred, but it is funny enough that it's worth telling.

Back then, there lived a Roman poet called Virgil who is considered to be one of Rome's greatest poets. He wrote significant works including *The Aeneid*, which is seen to have great historical and cultural value. Virgil was a successful man and was well compensated in his life for his writing and musings; he was also exceptionally clever. Virgil discovered that the government were intending to confiscate the lands belonging to the wealthy in order to provide living space for war veterans unless that land had a mausoleum (a building operating as a tomb) on it.

Virgil contemplated what to do. He noticed a house fly buzzing around his home and hatched a plot. He would keep the fly as a pet!

So, when the fly died shortly after its discovery, Virgil was in an almost catatonically miserable state; he simply *had* to commemorate the small insect's life somehow. So, he spent the modern-day equivalent of $1.6m on an extremely extravagant send-off.

The funeral is alleged to have had professional mourners crying, musicians playing sorrowful music, Roman celebrities were paid to attend, and lots of poetry was read. The crowning jewel was an expensive mausoleum housing the fly's tiny remains that, unfortunately, meant that Virgil's home was not eligible for confiscation, and he would remain in his lovely home with no negative but a housefly-shaped hole in his life and a vast hole in his wallet.

Again, if the story is true.

BAD LUCK TO BRING
A WOMAN ONBOARD, UNLESS
YOU'RE THIS WOMAN

Violet Jessop was an Argentinian woman born in the late 19th century to an Irish family. She moved to England at the age of 16 with her family after her father's death and left school shortly afterwards to become a stewardess aboard passenger ships. Stewardessing or Stewardessery (neither of these is a real term) was a relatively decent job in 1911 when Violet secured the work, as it was one of the few ways that women could reliably earn their own income at the time. She started her career aboard the *RMS Olympic*.

The journey was largely fine. The ship was the largest civilian liner of its day and was seen as a vessel of great luxury - it would have been an honor for Violet to be able to work aboard it. On September 20, 1911, the *Olympic* left port in Southampton and quickly collided with *HMS Hawke*, meaning it had to return to port. This was not seen as a major incident, and no one was injured or hurt, just a little shaken up. Most of us would then spend considerable hours of our life telling people about how "I survived an ocean liner collision once." Regrettably, Violet would have a different story to tell, as on 10 April 1912, she boarded a new ship…, *RMS Titanic*.

If you're not sure about the story of the *Titanic*, here's a quick recap; the *Titanic* was a luxury ocean liner carrying over 2,000 passengers that famously struck an iceberg on 14 April 1912, resulting in the deaths of more than half of its passengers and a hugely overrated movie. Jessop detailed in her memoirs how she was the model of civility as the boat began sinking in the Atlantic Ocean, trying to show people how to remain calm. She boarded a lifeboat and was rescued by the *RMS Carpathia* and eventually returned to Southampton. Most people would be so severely traumatized by this that they would probably never board a boat ever again. But not Violet! She took on work in 1914 as a stewardess for the British Red Cross to help in World War I and in 1916 was aboard the *HMHS Britannic*. Can you guess what happened to it?

The *Britannic* was the sister ship to the *Olympic* and the *Titanic*, so came from a line of great sinkers, and she made sure to follow suit expertly. On November 21, the boat suffered a colossal explosion, probably from a German sea mine, which led to the ship sinking in less than an hour. Remarkably, this resulted in the deaths of only 32 people. Jessop suffered a head injury but managed to survive to serve on even more liners in the 1920s and wrote memoirs of her bizarre times aboard these doomed vessels.

Jessop has earned the nickname *Miss Unsinkable* for good reason, though it makes me wonder: What sort of company hired her to be a stewardess with **that** record?

ST. LOUIS MARATHON MISHAPS

In 1904, the Olympics came to St Louis, America. It was tremendously exciting for the country to be the home of international sports for a summer. The Olympics were tied to the World Fair which, frankly, took most of the attention. 1904 was the third modern Olympics and with no easy way to broadcast it around the world, it just didn't have the pull that the World Fair had. The latter brought freak shows, mudslinging, and the "greased pole climb" to easily entertained audiences. The Olympics did have its share of interesting sporting moments, none more interesting and entertaining than the marathon - the main event designed to honor the Ancient Greek heritage of the Olympics and to recognize the greatest athletes in the world.

This marathon, however, was a little short of a disaster, albeit a very funny one.

The runner's stories are entertaining enough. To detail a few:

- Felix Carvajal, a Cuban runner, raised money in Cuba to compete in the Olympics by demonstrating his impressive running ability. He arrived in America and almost instantly lost all of his money in a dice game and had to hitchhike from New Orleans to St Louis. He ran in dress trousers that had been cut at the knee and street shoes.
- Fred Lorz was an American man who was a bricklayer in the daytime and trained at night.
- Ten Greeks competed who had never actually run a marathon before.
- Two South African men who were members of the Tsuana tribe ran barefoot.
- Some marathon runners from America were the favorites: A.L. Newton, Michael Spring, John Lordon, Thomas Hicks, and Sam Mellor.

The marathon is a medley of mismanagement and failure, and one could happily write 3000 words on the subject, so this will be a paired back and quicker version.

The racers all lined up to compete in this well-organized, carefully planned, and meticulously laid out course. Sorry, that's not quite right. The racers all lined up to compete in the world's worst organized marathon..., ever. The course was some 24 miles long and consisted of dusty roads, hills hundreds of feet high, traffic that hadn't been diverted, trains, and dog walkers. To further add agony to an already horrific course, the temperature was at 89 degrees Fahrenheit, and there were only two places where the racers could collect water as the organizer wanted to test the effects of purposeful dehydration on the human body.

Within the first mile, a runner called William Garcia collapsed with serious hemorrhaging from inhalation of dust and had to go to the hospital, almost dying in the process, while Len Tau of South Africa was chased drastically off course by wild dogs. Good start. Felix Carvajal was taking a leisurely pace; he stopped to talk to spectators and even visited an orchard and ate some apples. These caused severe stomach cramps, forcing him to have to stop for a small sleep. Fred Lorz collapsed with cramps at the nine-mile mark, so he decided that he'd catch a ride from someone driving an automobile for a mere 11 miles while he recovered. He emerged at the end of the race and was immediately declared the victor until someone pointed out that he'd mainly driven. He was then disqualified.

While all this was going on, Thomas Hicks was having the worst time of them all. He was struggling greatly by the 10-mile mark due to severe dehydration and..., well, every other aspect of the race. His two handlers decided to provide him with small doses of strychnine, a stimulating drug. Doping wasn't illegal at the time. The strychnine somewhat helped him as he limped and hobbled through the course. He begged for water several times but was only given further drugs or small amounts of French Brandy. Hicks suffered greatly, losing color and becoming limp as exhaustion set in. He learned that Lorz had been disqualified and desperately pushed himself through the last couple of miles while hallucinating and being refused any liquid beyond brandy.

He was eventually dragged over the finish line by his handlers. He lost eight pounds running the marathon.

So next time you're at the gym, huffing and puffing as you near the apex of your five-mile run, count yourself lucky you're not enduring Hicks' journey through hell.

FURIOUS WIDOWS MAKE GREAT SOLDIERS

Revenge is a dish best-served cold, or alternatively, it is best served via high explosive shells fired from the barrel of a T-34 tank. Either way, it can make for an exciting story.

Introducing Mariya, a Russian woman who was born in 1905 to a family of 10 children. Mariya worked as a telephone operator in her adult years and in 1925 she married a Soviet army officer called Ilya Oktyabrsky. Ilya's military career impacted Mariya greatly. She trained to drive vehicles, use weaponry, and joined the Military Wives Council. She had great pride in her marriage and loved Ilya greatly. So when, in 1941, Mariya was informed that her husband had been killed by the Germans *two years ago*, she became fueled by a consuming rage-grief cocktail and decided that she'd do something with the new fire in her belly.

Mariya sold off what she owned to raise funds as quickly as she could and bought a T-34 tank that she donated to the Soviet Army. There was a request along with this, however: the tank would only be donated if *she* could be the operator of the tank and name it *Fighting Girlfriend*. The defense committee agreed and enrolled Mariya in a five-month tank training program. In September 1943 she was posted to the 26th Guards Tank Brigade and was officially a part of the Red Army. Already, the story is pretty cool, but it gets even cooler when you find out what she did to the army that was responsible for her husband's death.

The story of Mariya Oktyabrskaya spread like wildfire through the ranks of the Red Army. Many scoffed at the notion of Mariya the tank driver, dismissing the whole thing as a ludicrous publicity stunt. Never dismiss the motivated and the angry - and especially don't dismiss someone who is motivated, angry, and has a tank. During the winter of 1943, Mariya specialized in destroying machine-gun nests and artillery guns. On multiple occasions, her tank was halted by the Germans, and she ignored orders and jumped out of her tank to fix the problem while under heavy fire. By the time 1944 rolled around, she was a sergeant, and her crew were seen as remarkably capable and deadly.

Unfortunately, Mariya saw her final battle in January 1944 in the Leningrad-Novgorod Offensive. Her tracks were damaged by a German anti-tank shell, and she hopped out of the tank to fix them under heavy fire. Her head was struck by shrapnel, and she lost consciousness. Two months later she succumbed to her injuries following a coma, passing on 15 March 1944. She was recognized as a *Hero of the Soviet Union* and her story exemplifies what happens when you make the wrong person angry.

SOMEONE'S GOT A CASE
OF THE MONDAYS!

People come up with all sorts of ways to get off work, don't they? Perhaps they'll lie about a sickness, or worse make up about going to a funeral, or even worse still, they commit a serious crime that gets them not one day, but 17 years off work!

Let's introduce Casey Fury, a shipyard worker who was working on the *USS Miami*, an actual, real, terrifying nuclear submarine. Casey was 25 in 2012, and it's safe to say that he probably wasn't *that* into his job. Casey was a painter and sand blaster, so wasn't in charge of the missiles or anything like that, but being on-site meant he had access to highly dangerous material.

So, it came to be that on 23 May, Casey told his bosses that he was suffering from anxiety that day and needed to leave work early, to which he was told a curt "no." What do you do at this stage? Perhaps plead with your bosses? Maybe you'd curse them under your breath but know that ultimately, you'll go home just having had a rubbish day. Well, neither of these options occurred to Casey. Instead, he decided to set a "small" fire in a bunk bed.

The resulting inferno took 12 hours for firefighters to tackle because of the extensive spread of the flames as well as the incredible heat that meant they could only stand in proximity to the blaze for mere minutes at a time. Seven people were injured and over $450m worth of damage was caused. The *USS Miami* was never used for its purpose again and after a relatively short investigation, Casey was found to be responsible for the destruction of the submarine.

In November 2012, he was arrested for two counts of arson…, oh yeah, he actually tried to set fire to the submarine again three weeks after the first fire to get out of work again. He was found guilty in March 2013 of arson alongside the injured workers and was sentenced to 17 years in prison as well as having to pay back $400m in reparations. (What's the point in a $400m fine? He's gone to prison at 25, he is never ever, paying that fine…ever.)

So next time you're thinking of blowing off work, just do it. Don't even think about blowing *up* work.

THE SAN DIEGO RAINMAKER

To call yourself *The Rainmaker* would be to name yourself as a superhero, or at least a very average wrestler. It's just as well then, that Charles Hatfield didn't call himself The Rainmaker, but rather he labeled himself as the *Moisture Accelerato*. We can all agree that's a name both boring and somehow revolting too.

But the thing about Hatfield is that he lived up to the name. Rainmaker, I mean, not moisture accelerator. He seemed able to make rain. In 1902, he developed a mixture of 23 chemicals that were combined in an evaporating tower. Hatfield claimed that the process attracted rain - and it seemed to work. His first job came in February of 1904 when Los Angeles ranchers agreed to pay him $50 for producing rain. He made a large evaporating tower, did his thing, and it apparently worked! Though the ranchers paid him $100 for his success, it is quite likely that this particular bout of rain was part of a storm that was already on the way. But either way, it didn't matter to the ranchers: they had their rain.

Hatfield continued to gather work through the early 20th century, collecting $1,000 from the Los Angeles government in 1905 and £1,100 for costs from Yukon miners despite failing to produce any rain in 1906. The big one came in 1915, however, when the San Diego city council, under pressure from citizens unhappy with the lack of rain and the dry reservoir, agreed to bring in the Rainmaker to produce rain.

The contract was agreed upon for $10,000 for between 40 and 50 inches of rain, though (and this is important) the contract wasn't signed. It was merely a verbal agreement. Hatfield built a tower and by January 1, 1916, he was ready to produce as he had been asked. On January 5, heavy rain started and grew day by day, becoming torrential and flooding quickly started. The rain continued until January 20, by which time riverbeds were overflowing, bridges had been destroyed, trains were marooned, and two dams were flowing over their barriers. But at least the rain was over.

Until January 22, when it started again. Five days later, the Lower Otay Dam broke. The devastation was vast and resulted in approximately 20 deaths.

Hatfield refused to acknowledge that he had done anything wrong and demanded his payment from the council. They refused unless he acknowledged that he was responsible for the damage, which amounted to $3.5m. Hatfield maintained that he had done as was requested as the reservoir was now full. True, but also Mr. Hatfield, 20 people have died, and you've destroyed half of San Diego!

The fact that there was no written contract meant that there was no clear answer to the suit. Legally there was no fee for Hatfield to claim and no contract that Hatfield had breached to sue him for. In 1938, the case eventually ended when two different courts decided that the rain was an act of God, and as such, it wasn't Hatfield's fault. But also, he was not deserving of any money.

Hatfield took his rain recipe, or moisture accelerant recipe (if you like) to the grave, dying at the age of 82 in 1958. Who knows if his method definitely worked, but he claimed hundreds of successful rain-making attempts in his lifetime.

THE GIFT OF
10 MILLION WOMEN

In the 20th century, China experienced rapid growth in all senses. After World War II, their population boomed, and they gradually became one of the dominant world economies. Given their communist government, established in 1949 by Mao Zedong, many Western countries refused to be diplomatically involved with China. This was the truest of America who refused to engage with China for decades.

In the 1970s, however, there were tentative discussions between the two countries, to examine whether or not there could be a peaceful and cooperative relationship. It was like trying to reconcile estranged siblings, years after they stopped talking because the younger one wouldn't take on any responsibility for their parents' 70th birthday celebrations. Henry Kissinger, Secretary of State and bombing enthusiast met with Mao Zedong to open diplomatic relations. The details of the discussion were revealed in the late 2000s as documents were declassified. Some of the details are numbered here in chronological order:

1. Chairman Mao laments that trade between the two countries was appalling and wished it would improve. He comments that "China is a very poor country" and that "we have an excess of women."
2. Chairman Mao suggests that China could send thousands of women to the US to instigate trade.
3. A silence permeates the room. Chairman Mao then throws the number "10 million" in the air, just to test what people think. The room fills with the sound of poorly-suppressed laughter.
4. Kissinger responds that the US has no quotas or tariffs for Chinese women. Diplomats and other important people continue to giggle. Kissinger then tries to move on by bringing

up the Soviet Union and the dangers they pose to international peace.

5. Mao is undeterred and brings the conversation back to women, saying, "…let them go to your place, they will create disasters. This way you can lessen our burdens. Do you want our Chinese women? We can give you 10 million."

6. Kissinger notes that the offer is improving.

7. Mao: "…they give birth to children and our children is too many." Kissinger says that "we will have to study" the proposition from Chairman Mao.

After these discussions, they considered international peace and the threat from the Soviet Union before deciding that they should scrap records of the meeting so as not to upset people. Thank God that they didn't. The style of bartering is certainly unique, and we'd all like to know where it goes from there.

10 million women to America, who respond with six million children, 300,000 horses, and a million cans of Coca-Cola?

SOMETIMES YOU JUST YEARN FOR A BABYBEL

Desperate times call for desperate measures, they always have. If you're desperate for a refreshing soda and the waiter says, "Sorry, we don't have Coca-Cola, but we have Pepsi," you may find yourself saying "Yes" even if it's obviously not the drink you wanted. Another example of this was observed in 1766 in Nottingham, UK when a historic and celebrated festival became the sight of a violent and furious riot in the wake of food shortages but especially because of some very expensive cheese.

1766 was a tough year in a long number of difficult years, most notably due to a punishing famine that drove up food prices drastically. Tensions were high, people were starving, and they were really quite fed up. The Goose Fair was gearing up to be somewhat of a miserable affair that year, which was a shame for the people of Nottingham. The Goose Fair had been an annual event for hundreds of years in the region, receiving a royal charter way back in 1284 that prevented other fairs in the county from competing with it. The fair acted as a place of enjoyment, revelry, selling and buying wares, and a generally positive community event (apart from the year that Graham brought up the neglected shared fence between him and his neighbor, probably).

This year, however, attention was drawn to cheese. In England, people's attention is often drawn to cheese, but in 1766 it was mainly because of the price. Large wheels of cheese were sold at the Goose Fair weighing in at about 110 pounds, about the same weight as six coffee tables. The price of these everlasting cheese wheels rose to a modern-day sum of approximately $200–250. Because of the rising prices, less cheese was being sold by producers, so there was going to be a large influx of cheese at the Goose Fair in 1766 and potentially at a slightly lower price.

News spread quickly that Lincolnshire merchants were intending on buying up most of the stock to re-sell, which infuriated the good people of Nottingham. They wanted Nottingham cheese to stay in Nottingham. When the merchants did indeed arrive to purchase the massive cheeses, a group of "rude lads" confronted them and a small fight broke out. People rushed in to steal the merchant's cheese and began to roll the wheels down the street, away from the merchants.

The violence spiraled and looting, destruction, and some general silly behavior broke out. Windows were smashed, fights continued, and cheese was continuously stolen throughout. The mayor pleaded for peace in vain and was quickly put out of commission as he attempted to stop a rolling cheese wheel, which easily bowled him over and continued past him without a cheesy care in the world.

The rioters refused to let cheese leave Nottingham and blockaded roads, robbed boats, and pillaged warehouses. There was some effort from the cheese owners to go and find their looted goods, but the magistrate refused point blank to provide a warrant for them to search houses for cheese. Some of the original "rude lads" were arrested on riot charges, which incited pure rage from the civilians who stormed the jail to free the "lads." The army was brought in, and they ended up shooting and killing one man.

The riot petered out as the cheese was removed from the city under military protection and the event became a singular example of riots in the year 1766.

THE GOLDFISH
GULPING FAD OF 1939

The great internet challenges of the 21st century are funny, silly, often dangerous, and produce thousands of copycat challenges. The Tide Pod challenge, Cinnamon challenge, Ice Bucket challenge, Planking, and the Harlem Shake, to name a few, have at some point absorbed the attention of thousands or millions of internet users taking part in something a bit silly. These internet fads are echoes of the crazy, outrageous fads from 1939 kickstarted by Lothrop Withington Jr., a Harvard freshman.

Lothrop told his friends excitedly that he'd once eaten a live fish. His friends didn't believe him and promised him $10 if he could repeat the bizarre feat. You show me a teenager who's turned down a stupid bet and I'll show you a teenager that is lying to you because you're his mum. On 3 March, Withington attracted an audience of students and a reporter from Boston (slow news day) as he held a three-inch-long goldfish in his hand and slowly lowered it into his mouth. He chewed a couple of times and swallowed.

Something like this in most instances is generally forgotten about with a bit of time and lives on in the memories of a group of friends. However, the fact that a reporter was present meant that the story spread rapidly. *Life* magazine covered it and soon after colleges around America were experiencing the craze of live goldfish swallowing. There were wild stories of great fish-swallowers, the most extreme of which was Joseph Deliberato from Clark University who allegedly swallowed a whopping 89 goldfish in *one sitting*.

Eventually, State Senator George Krapf filed a bill to "preserve the fish from cruel and wanton consumption." With further panic from animal rights groups becoming very public, greater attention was paid to the craze. In the UK, you can even be fined for taking the challenge on to this day. There has been a slight resurgence of the craze on the internet in recent years, but if nothing else, the challenge can be seen as one of the original viral crazes, witch-hunting obviously being the first.

And it could be argued that sushi didn't first become a craze in the 1980s after all.

THE EGYPTIAN PREGNANCY TEST

Discovering that you are pregnant is a wonderful, magical moment that many people spend their lives looking forward to…, while others dread it.

If you want to find out whether or not you're pregnant, then you can take a pregnancy test purchased at your favorite pharmacy, approach a local witch/wizard/prophet if you trust them, or simply cross your fingers and pray. Throughout history, humans have tested whether someone is pregnant with varying degrees of success. In 1927, an experiment was run that involved injecting the woman's urine into a mouse and basing conclusions on the mouse's reaction. The 19th-century methods focused almost entirely on watching to see if symptoms of pregnancy arose, while the Middle Ages saw the rise of "p*** prophets" who would examine the urine of a lady and mix it with wine to observe certain reactions (which may have worked, though they wouldn't have known why). But one of the earliest forms of pregnancy test that we know about was used in Ancient Egypt and carries a success rate of around 70%, which isn't bad for 1350 BCE!

The test was simple, and the most compelling evidence of it is from a papyrus that describes the test in perfect detail. The woman in question is presented with two sacks, one filled with barley seed and the other with wheat seed. She is then to urinate on the two sacks, and "if the barley grows, it means a male child. If the wheat grows, it means a female child. If both do not grow, she will not bear at all."

The test was itself tested for its efficacy in 1963 and that is when the test was determined to be 70% accurate in predicting pregnancy. It is completely inaccurate when it comes to predicting the sex of the baby, but otherwise, it was actually rather reliable, which makes it another item to add to the list of impressive feats from Ancient Egyptians. The reason it works is likely that the level of estrogen coursing through a pregnant woman would be present in their urine and causes the seed to sprout. None of this would have occurred to the Ancient people, but it's amazing that they still managed to develop a reliable system to know if a baby was on the way.

The real question is how on earth did they decide to perform this test in the first place? "Oh, you haven't had an accident, have you?! All over the barley and the wheat! Wait…what's going on there?"

THE 66 CE MOONING

The great bottom flash, known as "mooning," is a fantastic form of human communication. What better way informs someone that you find them utterly repugnant, a true rotter, a completely grotesque individual of cataclysmic proportions than by showing them your complete posterior? Well, it could be argued that simply telling them that you have a problem is definitely more mature, but the signal that you give to people via the unsubtle moon transcends all language. The history of the humble moon is an interesting one that can be traced back throughout our time on Earth.

The word itself seemed to have emerged from 17th-century England when showing your bum was called 'exposing to moonlight'. Presumably, most mooning was done at night when your chance of being spotted is less likely. The early explorers of the Atlantic wrote that the Etchemin tribe practiced mooning when they spotted Western sailors in the 16th century. In 1204 at the Siege of Constantinople, part of the Fourth Crusade, the Greeks flaunted their cheeks to the Crusaders from the walls of Constantinople, revolting the invaders.

The earliest known mooning comes from those pinnacles of creation and culture - the Romans. We date it to approximately 66 CE and it comes from writing by Flavius Josephus, a prominent historian and military leader. The mooning was performed during the First Roman-Jewish War in Jerusalem. An outspoken Roman soldier decided to upset the Jewish people by mooning pilgrims at the Jewish temple who were there for Passover. Flavius writes that as well as flashing his backside, he spoke several rude insults that "you might expect upon such a posture." The response was absolute fury from the Jewish pilgrims and resulted in a riot that culminated in the deaths of some 10,000 Jews. Certain questions arise as to whether we could consider this mooning to be a war crime.

It's very likely that the insult of a well-timed moon goes back further than this, perhaps to the earliest homo sapiens, but that would be pure conjecture. Many intelligent people wouldn't like to admit it, but you know it now: the moon is a powerful move and is one that perhaps, in some way, bonds us all together.

SO, HOWL DO I SIGN UP?

Picture a pug. Now laugh a bit because they look a little funny. Now consider what words come to mind when you think of the personality of a pug..., did you come up with:

Loyalty, Steadiness, Trustworthiness

If you did, then you would have been a great candidate to become a member of the *Order of the Pug,* a short-lived secret society founded in 18th-century Bavaria by a group of Roman Catholics. The society was founded after Catholics were banned from joining any Freemason groups. It was founded around 1740 and managed to stay completely secret and exclusive for a whopping five years until its secrets were exposed in a book published in Amsterdam. There's a lack of written material about what the Order of the Pug went on to do or what the general achievements or aims were, but we do know a bit about their rituals and behaviors.

Members called themselves "mops," the German word for "pug" and the masters (one female and male per sect or lodge) were called "grand pugs." Initiation was a convoluted affair, with there being many aspects to receiving admission into the group. Total novices put on a dog collar and scratched at the door of the lodge to be let in. Once in, they'd be put on a leash and led around the room nine times while the mops barked at them. If you weren't dissuaded from being part of the strange group at this stage, then nothing was going to stop you!

As the initiation continued, the novices had to kiss a porcelain pug's bottom under the tail, in the "business section" as it were, to show their dedication to the order. Shortly after this, a hand was placed on a rapier (sword) if you were a man or a mirror (a shiny thing you look in) if you were a woman and vows of dedication would be repeated. Finally, the blindfold was removed as the initiate was told to "see the light" and the new mop was greeted with a room full of order members holding a rapier or mirror in one hand and a pug in the left.

It is a bizarre ritual and though the groups were short-lived, it's likely that they were active as late as 1902 in Lyon, France. If you ask the average person what they thought of the group in the 19th century they'd have told you that the group were *barking mad*.

IMAGINE THE HANGOVER...

The days following the end of World War II in the European Theater were by all accounts a time of unbelievable joy. May 8 is still marked and celebrated every year as VE Day. People embraced, cheers were cheered, and speeches were given:

> *"My dear friends, this is your hour. It's a victory of the great British nation as a whole. We were the first, in this ancient island, to draw the sword against tyranny."*

For the Soviet Russians, however, the victory was celebrated differently. Stalin refused to acknowledge May 8 as a victory day for Russia as he hadn't been present to sign the agreement in France. Essentially, he was having a bit of a tantrum. Instead, their celebrations lay on May 9, and it was quite the scene of revelry. Citizens took to the streets for a 22-hour-long party. Stalin wasn't quite as interested. When congratulated over the telephone by Deputy Khrushchev, he snapped back, "why are you bothering me? I am working."

The Russian people had suffered greatly during World War II. The Eastern Front was home to absolute barbarity for six years. For the people of Russia, the relief was felt by all (unless you're Stalin, or I suppose a prisoner) and the party seems to have been legendary. There are several reports that many of the celebrating civilians were dressed in their pajamas for the duration of the day-long party. There were processions, much cheering, music, dancing, eating, and importantly, lots and lots and lots of vodka to be drunk.

For many Russians, vodka is *the* national alcoholic beverage. It's traditionally made from fermenting grain and potato, producing a powerful alcohol that in Eastern Europe is drunk quite consistently. Russia's Victory Day included so much vodka drinking that the Russian Federation actually managed to completely run out. One can only imagine that the collective hangover on May 10 could be considered the world's most serious self-induced chemical attack!

77

IT'S CHEAP AS CHIMPS
TO EMPLOY HIM

You know when someone tells you, "a trained monkey could do that job better than you, you odorous little idiot." No? Well, people do say it, okay! It may not be a nice thing to holler at someone, but if you do hear it, you can bring up the tale of Jack the baboon and they'll feel quite the fool for trying to insult you. Or they'll think you're a massive nerd and laugh at you.

Jack was a baboon (don't know if you knew that yet) who lived in South Africa in the late 19th century. The baboon was bought in the 1880s by a man called James Edwin Wide who was impressed after visiting a market and witnessing him operating an oxcart. He bought the baboon, named him Jack and so started a successful working relationship with Jack as his assistant. James needed help as he'd lost both of his legs in a work-related accident. The first thing he did was train Jack to wheel him to work in a small trolley as well as complete some domestic chores like sweeping and trash removal.

Jack was destined for bigger things, however; he accompanied James to work and observed him performing his job as a signalman. The trains would *toot* their horns a certain number of times to signal that the tracks needed to be changed to a given direction. Amazingly, Jack watched and learned how to do this, meaning that James soon didn't have to do any real work himself! James reportedly would sit in his cabin stuffing animals while Jack performed the task dexterously.

A train passenger, on their journey passing the cabin, was outraged to see a baboon operating the levers rather than a human and complained to the authorities. The authorities decided that they'd test Jack, rather than order James not to bring a BABOON into work. Incredibly, Jack performed perfectly, and the authorities decided that he was good to continue working. Railway superintendent George B. Howe said:

"Jack knows the signal whistle as well as I do, also every one of the levers."

Jack would never make a mistake while working for the company and was paid in beer and 20 cents a week (don't ask what he did with the money) before passing away in 1890 from tuberculosis. Jack's skull is now on display at Albany Museum in Grahamstown, South Africa.

Goes to show that if you TRAIN the monkey well enough, being a TRAINed monkey isn't so bad after all.

MID-LIFE CRISIS: RED FERRARI OR PLUNDERIN' BOOTY?

People often try desperately to reclaim their youth in their mid-life. Nowadays, that includes such stereotypical things as - an expensive holiday, a fast car, a motorbike, gambling, a new and younger partner, hair transplants, poorly fitting skinny jeans, playing Van Halen loudly, starting to play the guitar, and so on and so forth. But how about throwing your whole life to the side and turning to piracy?

Well, that's what Stede Bonnet, a professional soldier and professional moron, did. Bonnet was born in Barbados in 1688 and spent his life living in comfort and wealth, coming from an English landowning family, and inheriting a lot of that land himself. He spent most of his time travelling around the sugar plantation he owned with his wife, making a very decent living, and just generally being well-off. Then, seemingly without warning, in 1717 he turned to piracy.

No one is sure why he did this; perhaps he was bored, or perhaps he'd had a conflict with his wife and wanted to end his marriage. Either way, the man was heading into his thirties and in an age where life expectancy sat between 30–40, he was very much in the "late-mid-life crisis" area of his life. Bonnet is often referred to as "The Gentleman Pirate" due to his wealthy background and also because he was awful at being a pirate.

First, he purchased his own boat with 10 cannons called *Revenge* and hired a crew of seamen from the area. Yes, it had started with him buying a boat. Which no decent pirate does. You *steal* the boat. He paid his crew very well, which helped keep them on his side because he had no sailing experience nor any experience in leading a naval crew. They managed to do a small amount of plundering and capturing of ships, but by all accounts, Bonnet had very little to do with that.

Bonnet encountered Blackbeard, the most feared pirate on the seven seas, who boarded the *Revenge* and spoke with Bonnet. He quickly saw

Bonnet for what he was: a useless sailor but pleasant enough. They set sail together and got on well. Blackbeard easily convinced Bonnet to give up command of the *Revenge* as he had no idea what he was doing. Instead, Blackbeard offered, Bonnet could stay on Blackbeard's ship *Queen Anne's Revenge*. He sort of accepted and became a passenger to the infamous criminal.

Blackbeard eventually tricked Bonnet, stole his possessions and money, and left him on an island with a skeleton crew and the *Revenge*. Bonnet re-took control of the ship and, after seeking an official pardon for his pirate days, went back to attempting to plunder and steal. His days didn't last long, however, and Bonnet was soon captured in October 1718 by pirate hunter William Rhett.

Bonnet was executed in November 1718 for piracy and must go down as someone who threw it all away. He had an easy life and gave that up only to become one of the worst pirates of all time.

HIDE AND DON'T GO SEEK

The Tower of London is one of the oldest landmarks in England. Founded in 1066, the castle has received near-constant amendments ever since. It has been a royal residence, prison, execution site, museum, armory, and the site of one of the most long-lasting mysteries in English history.

The mystery centers around two princes, Edward V and his brother Richard who disappeared in 1483 at the ages of 12 and nine, respectively. The boys' father, Edward IV died quickly after an illness struck him in Easter of 1483, though he had survived long enough to add some amendments to his will including making arrangements for his sons. They would go into the care of his brother, the Duke of Gloucester, who would later be known as King Richard III.

It seems likely that Edward didn't know his brother as well as he'd thought. He probably assumed that Richard would raise the children carefully and with love, given that he had a future king in his charge. Instead, Richard almost instantly placed the boys into the Tower of London for "their protection." Richard maintained that there would be people looking to harm the boys given their royal status, so he made sure that they were always kept an eye on by guards at the Tower, again for "their own protection."

Despite this amazing so-called protection that the boys were under, and the undoubted levels of care and love that their uncle had provided them, they were never seen or heard of again. Many, for *some* reason, seem to blame Richard. Probably because he was jealous of having never been king and after the mysterious disappearance, he was crowned King Richard III. So, there is a small amount of evidence to suggest that he *might* have been responsible.

The fact remains, however, that we don't know what happened to the boys and we can't 100% say that Richard was responsible (although it seems like he was, right?). In 1674, the skeletal remains of two young boys were found beneath a staircase in the White Tower of the site. There has been some testing of the remains in the 20th century, but nothing that identifies anyone for certain.

What is for sure is that the whole thing smells mightily fishy, and that's not just the smell emanating from the staircase.

"HOUSTON, DO YOU COPY?"
"...WOOF"

The Space Race! Excitement! Gravity-defying science! Astronauts! Monkeys!

After World War II, the world was gripped by space, its magical wonders, and its countless, infinite mysteries. The mid-20th century saw great leaps in space exploration and technology with notable moments including the first person on the Moon, the first human technology on Mars, and eventually, the launch of the International Space Station. All these great leaps for humankind were possible through constant efforts by scientists all over the world - and a few unsuspecting animals.

The first animals sent into outer space were a group of fruit flies. There had been no confirmation of how radiation in space would impact humans. Fruit flies share 75% of their genetic makeup with humans - there's a great insult: "you're three-quarters a useless bug that dies within a day!" So, anyway, that's why the flies were sent into orbit. They were then examined once the capsule had returned, providing valuable information about the radiation from space.

The first animal to make an orbital spaceflight was a very famous little poochie by the name of *Laika*, who was launched into space by the Soviet Union in 1957. Laika passed several canine tests for space flight and her calm personality and doggedness (ha!) made her the best dog possible. Excitement was high for her flight and for what could be learned from it, but Laika regrettably died due to a lack of oxygen and temperature control. There's a monument to her in Russia outside Star City.

There have been many other animals, including 32 monkeys who stole a rocket and sent it into orbit never to be seen again. Only joking! They were each in their own experiments, but there's something very pleasing about the notion of a series of monkey astronauts. The most recent primate in space went in 2013, launched by Iran.

The first animals to orbit the moon were two tortoises, supplied with sustenance and launched on September 15, 1968. Seven days later, they returned to Earth and managed to survive re-entry. They were interviewed about their experiences but regrettably had very little to say (again, a joke). In 1973, a spider called Arabella spun the first web in space to answer the question of whether or not spiders could spin webs in zero gravity. In 2007, a cockroach gave birth to 33 cockroaches aboard a satellite, becoming the first creature to do so in space. Everyone celebrated, then instantly said, "Ew!"

There are more to study, but it's worth appreciating that the only reason that space travel has come so far is due to our scaley, furry, feathered, and buggy friends that went before.

"I DO HOPE WE DIDN'T MISS ANYTHING IMPORTANT"

DISCLOSURE: THE FOLLOWING BROADCAST IS A FICTIONAL ACCOUNT BASED ON THE POPULAR NOVEL *WAR OF THE WORLDS* FROM 1898, ENJOY AT YOUR LEISURE.

A warning like this is probably one that you'd have wanted to hear before listening to the now-infamous 1938 radio broadcast of the hit novel *The War of the Worlds*. The novel is about an alien invasion that causes widespread death and devastation across England before the aliens are, in the end, wiped out by bacteria.

Orson Welles, now seen as a genius and pioneer in cinematic and entertainment history, helped orchestrate a radio broadcast of the book, which was carried out innovatively. The broadcast was done as though the invasion was *actually* happening at that moment in time! The first half an hour featured an evening of normal broadcasting that was intermittently interrupted by urgent news bulletins. Before long, the reports became more chaotic, culminating in accounts of aliens emerging from an alien spacecraft before the panic was heard and the feed cut dead.

Importantly, there *was* a disclosure at the start of the broadcast like the one above, warning people that the show was not real and was purely for entertainment purposes. The problem is that not everyone heard this. If you weren't listening to the very first part of the broadcast, perhaps busy or listening to another channel that wasn't *CBS Radio*, then it sounded like actual aliens had invaded Earth! Which is exactly what some people thought was happening.

Newspapers reported that chaos had broken out across America as thousands panicked, resulting in suicides, looting, and violence. Orson Welles later stated that some civilians were out for blood; his blood:

"After the broadcast, as I tried to get back to the St. Regis where we were living, I was blocked by an impassioned crowd of news people looking for blood, and the disappointment when they found I wasn't hemorrhaging."

The broadcast has gone down in infamy as well as hilarity, as an example of how gullible people can be. Historians have since confirmed that, in reality, basically no one was fooled and instead most simply enjoyed a fun show. And the phrase "most" is used very lightly as only 2% of radio listeners at the time were even listening to the show! Most were listening to *The Chase and Sanborn Hour*.

We'd better hope if aliens do invade, people aren't listening to the news on the radio, or no one will believe it.

THE BEST WORST JOB
IN ALL THE LAND

Picture the scene: It's 1519 in Tudor England. Henry VIII is the king and is spending lavish amounts of money on wars, feasts and on servants and musicians for his court, which means he might be willing to give *you* some money to come and work for him! How exciting! What would you like to do? Perhaps be a chef? A drummer? A humorous jester telling jokes about political goings-on across Europe? You'll be paid handsomely and perhaps even climb into the upper classes of Tudor England. A letter arrives for you, and you tear it open. It reads:

> *"King Henry formally invites you to join his court in an important role as His Majesty's Groom of the Stool. Arrive at Hampton Court some time after breakfast to begin your new role."*

Your jaw drops open; you can't believe it. You are going to be the *GROOM OF THE STOOL!?* You are going to be the King's actual, real, bum-wiper. Lucky you!!

The Groom of the Stool was a prestigious job in Tudor England, partly because of the comparatively high wage you were paid and also due to your closeness to the King. And yes, just to be clear, the Groom of the Stool's job was to clean up the King's back passage after he had been to the lavatory.

The obvious question is "Why can't the King clean his own bottom?" but, truthfully, the job is a bit of an easy win. You're not required to do the work very often, and yes it may be unpleasant, particularly after a night of feasting on four different meats and gallons of wine and ale, but you get a lot of privileges when you're working so closely with the head honcho. William Compton, Henry's first Groom of the Stool was given vast amounts of land and offices for his services. He brought in about £2,000 per year, which is the modern-day equivalent of about

£1m. (I don't know about you, but I, the writer, would happily wipe a bum for £1m per year!)

Next time you're on the porcelain throne, think about whether you have the funds to hire someone (on minimum wage, perhaps) to give your area a bit more attention.

WHO WANTS SECONDS?

Pies have long been adored in Britain; the delicate simplicity of the hearty dish has won out for centuries. Some sort of protein, vegetables, and sauce inside of an edible pastry container is an easy win for 99% of British people, even today. One particular type of pie hasn't held the test of time, however, the now-forgotten Lamprey Pie.

If you're unsure of what a lamprey is, it's time to feel a bit uneasy. Lampreys are a type of fish that evolved over 200 million years ago to what they are today and belongs to a family of jawless fish. It looks quite a lot like an eel, possessing a large sucking disc filled with nasty-looking teeth. It feeds on its prey by latching onto an animal and drawing the blood and tissue from the unfortunate victim.

This bizarre parasite was seen as a delicacy by the upper classes and royalty in England until the mid-19th century. King Henry I, had such a voracious appetite for the lamprey that he was said to have died due to eating too many of them! Some historians reckon it was poorly prepared lamprey that killed him rather than too much, though Charles Dickins himself wrote of the King's untimely fate in his book *A Child's History of England*.

The pie containing this special ingredient involves an oddly convoluted process of preparation. The lampreys were cooked in a sort of syrup inside the pie. The crust would be ceremoniously opened, and the syrup mixed with wine and spices before being spooned onto thick slices of white bread. The lamprey was removed from the pie, sliced thinly, and laid on top of the sodden bread and eaten.

There was a status thing to eating lamprey; they're not all that easy to find. But presumably, it must have tasted alright as well. Although it definitely can't have looked any good.

TOO DELICIOUS FOR THEIR OWN GOOD

The Giant Tortoise is a majestic creature that has managed to outlast prehistoric beasties like mammoths and saber-toothed tigers by finding refuge in the Galapagos Islands in the Pacific Island. The islands are famous for the visit of the bearded, God-doubting, world-rocker Charles Darwin in the 19th century. Darwin used the tortoises he found there to help prove his Theory of Evolution, by showing how minute differences can occur in animals. He also likely would have, given the chance, had them in their own shell-like bowl as a soup, perhaps served with a crusty white bread roll.

That's because Galapagos Giant Tortoises are notoriously tasty. However, the tortoises are now a protected species. Not even Gordon Ramsay is permitted to create a Giant Tortoise Wellington (no matter how much he begs - leave it alone, Gordon). We have an idea of how they taste from 17th-century explorer William Dampier:

> *"[they are] extraordinarily large and fat, and so sweet, that no pullet [hen] eats more pleasantly."*

Paul Chambers, a modern writer who wrote about the plight of the Giant Tortoise, lamented that these sorts of descriptions were very common. In fact, the so-called scientific descriptions of these tortoises read like restaurant reviews until the 1800s. There were many attempts to bring tortoises back to England throughout the centuries for research and curiosity purposes. They were capable of withstanding sea travel, so could live aboard a ship as they awaited their munchy death.

By 1830, an estimated 100,000 Galapagos Giant Tortoises had been taken and, probably, eaten by the British. When Darwin himself arrived in 1835, he took 30 tortoises back with him *for food*. A snack! He later regretted how he and the crew had supped on the slow creatures, writing that they'd eaten "the most important specimens on board the Beagle."

He was supposed to be a scientist! Try telling me that when he's got bits of tortoise in his gray beard.

THE WORST THING SINCE NON-SLICED BREAD

World War II brought many difficulties to citizens living at home as soldiers fought in Europe and Asia. Resources were spread thinly and much of what was available had to go toward fighting the war. If you were one of those who didn't go to fight, then you faced severe rationing in most countries as worldwide trade collapsed. Many housewives (and it was 99% of housewives) had to find new ways to feed the family while keeping meals varied and with adequate nutrition.

What was being rationed changed a lot depending on what was in short supply, though often it was meat and seasonal vegetables. Machinery and factories were repurposed by governments to manufacture munitions, preventing the production of some food products. In 1943, the US placed a full-on ban on one product to ensure that resources weren't being thrown about willy-nilly (*willus-nillus*, if you're speaking Latin). In January the government decided that, among many things, sliced bread was now not allowed to be sold in America. Take one moment to guess why before you read on....

????

It was due to the wrapping that the bread came in. If you slice bread in advance, then you need to use more wrapping to keep the bread contained and together, whereas a full loaf of bread is easily picked up and transported with no wrapping. As well as wax paper being preserved for other uses, the reasoning for the decision from the Secretary of Agriculture was also to avoid wasting steel for the production of bread-slicing machines. The country needed every resource possible, and it was seen as a luxury that could be given up, though not everyone felt that way.

Time Magazine reported that there was widespread frustration from housewives who were suddenly having to battle with a serrated bread knife for the first time. Stories of toasters refusing un-even, door-wedge-shaped slices were abundant and perhaps for the first time, the reality of the war was coming home. Quoting from *Time Magazine*, February 1, 1943:

> *"To U.S. housewives it was almost as bad as gas rationing - and a whale of a lot more trouble."*

DO WE NAME IT CORNHUB?

It's worth mentioning at this stage that this book is not sponsored by anything or anyone and the following story is in no way a paid-advertisement..., obviously, this is what the book would say if it was presenting a paid-advertisement and didn't want anyone to know. But it isn't..., yet.

When you're a child, your parents may very well bundle you into the back of a car somewhat early in the morning with the promise of a surprise trip. The excitement courses through you and visions emerge in your mind as you consider the possibilities. Where could we be going? The beach? A water park? Disneyland?! No, no it's far better than any of those dull suggestions:

"Kids! We're going to the South Dakota Corn Palace!"

So, it's not the most thrilling-sounding place, but to be fair, its real name is *The World's Only Corn Palace*, which is a much better name.

The Corn Palace in Mitchell, South Dakota is an interesting building that was designed in 1892 to celebrate a successful corn harvest. The Palace is best known for its intricate, corn-related murals adorning the building made from ears of corn, paint, and thousands of nails. Each year, local artists work hard on designs to spice up the palace and it receives some 500,00 visitors who come predominantly to gawk at the a-Maize-ing works of art.

The World's Only Corn Palace is really a bit of a misleading name. During the late 19th century, over 30 palaces are believed to have been constructed in cities and towns across Midwest America. It just so happens that Michell's is the only one that remains intact.

Different events are held at the Palace, so if you're in the area (and I mean in the area, don't go out of your way), then why not go and see this bizarre celebration of corn?

SOMETIMES, CHEATERS DO PROSPER

Bartenders are interesting people. You meet some who are experts in the craft of mixology, some who are earning money on the side while they chase something else, and some who have that wild look in their eye, like they could do anything. Dan Saunders is without a doubt in the last category. In 2011, Dan was having some zesty beverages at a local bar in the evening, when he decided to withdraw some cash (for an undisclosed reason) from the nearest ATM. The ATM acted strangely. To be fair, it was 1 a.m. and its customer was acting weird, so I don't blame the ATM here. But after the machine didn't initially allow Dan to access his money, he did some shifting around on his online banking and the ATM ended up giving him $200 in cash. Dan noticed that the ATMs were offline and through some moving around of cash on his phone, he could magic up any figure he wanted and remove it from the ATM.

Dan withdrew thousands in cash that first night, brain alive with the possibilities of what he could do with a seemingly unlimited amount of money. What comes to your mind? Yachts? Partying? Trips to Paris? Well, Dan did all of that and more. Over the course of four and a half months, Dan managed to accrue $1.6m and he SPENT IT. It's the stuff dreams are made of! I am certain that Dan can't go into the full spectrum of where the money went, legally, but he did comment on how differently people treat you when you have cash to splash. People offered him new money-making schemes (in my experience, anyone at a bar telling you about a money-making scheme should be completely ignored - I'm still out $60 on that sausage re-selling scheme) and women seemed more interested than they had been before.

Dan eventually turned himself in, mostly out of guilt and presumably because EVENTUALLY he would have been caught. Probably. He served a brief prison sentence of one year and some community service afterwards. This goes to show that cheaters…, could absolutely, prosper. Dan could have gotten away with this without a shadow of a doubt. If he'd moved his money to a bank in Switzerland and then made a series of small investments on the stock exchange as well as in property in mainland European cities, he would have lived easy forever…, not that I've ever thought about doing that. Dan now works as a bartender and he says, through gritted teeth, that he believes he made the right decision in the end.

I wonder what you would do. (We know exactly what you'd do, you can see it in your eyes.)

DO WE THINK
HE'S DEAD YET?

What do you know of 1910s Russia? Nothing? Thank God for that, otherwise you'd probably already know the story and legend of Ra-Ra-Rasputin.

Decades before Boney M.'s classic song by the same name, there lived the real man Grigori Rasputin who had an extraordinary life by anyone's metric. Rasputin gained a reputation in Russia after he acted as a mystic healer for the Royal Family's son Alexei, who suffered from hemophilia (a rare blood disease). Rasputin was a suspicious character. He cut a daunting figure standing at six foot four inches and had intense, cold, blue eyes that seemed to mystify people who stared into them. Many people thought that he could hypnotize others, and this was why the Royals had him in their employ. A lot of the suspicion came mainly from his relationship with Tsarina Alexandra. Many people thought (and still think) that Rasputin was conducting a lustful affair with the Queen and endangered the sanctity of Russia by doing so.

Rasputin is known for being a party animal, indulging in drink, drugs, and fornication on an almost impossible level. Interestingly, the Museum of Erotica in St. Petersburg supposedly houses Rasputin's penis, pickled in a jar, though this isn't verified. There's great speculation over whether it's even human, but the museum won't allow anyone to test it for some reason.

By 1916, Russia was two years and several million casualties into World War I, and there was a general sense of trepidation and fed-upness in the country. In 1917, the country would brutally overthrow its monarchy in favor of communism. Before that though, in December 1916, some decided that they'd get rid of the scary, potentially evil Rasputin. A group of Russian noblemen decided to carry out the plot to save the reputation of the royal family who seemed to be under his wicked spell. The account of his death is as bizarre as the accounts of his life and is heavily disputed but goes as this:

Rasputin was lured to nobleman Felix Yusupov's palace on December 30 and ushered into the basement before being offered tea and cakes laced with cyanide, a lethal poison. Rasputin indulged and was surprisingly totally fine. Yusupov was aghast as Rasputin asked for a glass of wine. He sank three glasses. The wine was also poisoned, but when Rasputin showed no signs of discomfort, Yusupov decided at 2:30 a.m. to be a bit more certain, so shot Rasputin in the chest. He collapsed to the ground before later leaping up and attacking Yusupov. The noblemen were chased out into the courtyard and continued shooting at Rasputin before he finally collapsed into a snowbank. He was wrapped in cloth and dumped into the Malaya Nevka River and found a few days later.

That account was reported by Felix Yusupov himself in his memoirs and is *heavily* disputed, but it is fun to imagine Rasputin as the Russian Terminator, refusing to back down and refusing to die. Rumor has it that he still stalks the earth to this day, looking for his severed penis. No one will tell him of its fate.

DOUBLE THE DIAPERS
AND DOUBLE THE CRYING

Sumo is an ancient and revered sport that requires lifetime devotion to succeed. Many Westerners laugh openly at the spectacle of two very large men in ceremonial underwear slapping each other in a chalk circle, but the rituals of the sport are carefully maintained and respected in Japan. Sumo wrestlers are highly respected. Their fighting style is generally seen as being tough to perform and the career is difficult to stay competitive in. That is, apart from one form of annual match-up known as the Naki Sumo Crying Baby Festival.

These match-ups involve two massive sumo wrestlers, each holding a baby. The babies are the competitors, not the wrestlers, with the first crying baby declared the winner. Many adults would probably also cry if they were held by a big, burly sumo wrestler, so the battle doesn't go on for long before the babies begin to wail. It may seem a bit strange, but the festival actually has roots in Japanese culture that dates back approximately 400 years.

It's believed that this type of match-up began because shrieking babies were thought to ward off evil spirits and demons. Each location's rules around the crying differ, but generally, a good, strong, loud cry is an indication of a healthy baby and one who will grow well over the years. If both babies cry at the same time, then a referee is given the difficult job of deciding which baby cried the best. For many adults, this may very well be a worse job than the infamous Groom of the Stool mentioned earlier in this book. There are few sounds more irritating to adults than the sound of a wailing baby; imagine what it would be like to judge which baby is crying better than the other!

THREE LIVES DOWN, SIX LEFT

We love an animal with seemingly supernatural abilities. There have been reports of cats sensing when people are near death, dogs who refuse to leave their owners' graves, and hamsters who aren't terrified of everything they've ever come across. All supernatural fluffs. Though impressively, a small black-and-white cat by the name of Oscar trumps most animals and people with his incredible, oddly spooky feat accomplished during World War II that earned him the nickname "Unsinkable Sam."

Oscar's origins are largely unknown. He probably belonged to a German soldier and was brought aboard the battleship *Bismarck* in 1941 for Operation Rheinübung, which set out to prevent shipping from reaching the United Kingdom. After a little more than a week at sea, the *Bismarck* became embroiled in an aggressive sea battle that saw it destroyed along with 2,000 seamen onboard. It was a brutal assault and few stood a chance of surviving. Yet found floating on a board in the ocean was little Oscar (presumably looking a bit startled and downright miserable, after all, cats hate getting wet).

He was picked up by the *HMS Cossack*. The crew first named him Oscar there, being code for 'Man Overboard' in the International Code of Signals.

Oscar's career aboard the *Cossack* unfortunately was cut short after only a few months. The ship carried out envoy duties predominantly and was eventually struck by a German submarine while journeying from Gibraltar to the United Kingdom in October 1941. The explosion was devastating to the ship, making it completely unsuitable for further operation while also killing off 157 members of its crew. Fear not, Oscar was fine. The remaining crew joined the *HMS Legion* including Oscar and this was when he was first dubbed "Unsinkable Sam."

After reaching Gibraltar, Oscar joined the aircraft carrier *HMS Ark Royal* where he sailed without incident...

...is what would be written if this was a lie. Unfortunately, the *Ark Royal* was torpedoed in November 1941 and the carrier eventually sunk some 30 miles from Gibraltar. Luckily, only one crew member died during the sinking and, especially lucky for our story, that crewman was not Oscar. Bizarrely, the ships that the crew (including Sam) were picked up by, the *HMS Legion* and *HMS Lightning*, were also sunk in 1942 and 1943, respectively.

But by 1942, Sam had found more permanent lodgings in Belfast, in a home known as the *Home for Sailors*. He died in 1955 and has a portrait in the National Maritime Museum in Greenwich.

Perhaps Unsinkable Sam isn't a great name. After all, every boat he ever boarded seemed to sink. Perhaps Oscar was just busy proving that cats really do have nine lives.

THE UNLUCKIEST
LUCKIEST MAN EVER

The year is 1945. Tsutomu Yamaguchi designs oil tankers for Mitsubishi Heavy Industries. His life is perfectly normal, though Japan is still at war and the dangers that come with the global conflict are still very much present. He had been on a three-month-long business trip during the summer with some colleagues and found himself in the city of Hiroshima on August 6, 1945. At approximately 8 a.m. Yamaguchi was walking along the docks when he witnessed one of the rarest and most grotesque moments in all human history.

The American bomber called *Enola Gay* had just passed overhead and dropped the first-ever targeted nuclear bomb, approximately two miles away from where he stood. The bomb dropped on Hiroshima killed around 80,000 people almost instantly and Yamaguchi recalls seeing:

"A great flash in the sky, and I was blown over."

Yamaguchi was thrown to the ground with ruptured eardrums, temporary blindness, and serious radiation burns. He went to find the colleagues he was due to meet and discovered that they had also survived the explosion. They all spent the night in an air-raid shelter and breathed a sigh of relief for a moment. To have been witness to the Hiroshima explosion and lived to tell the tale is lucky, extremely lucky. It's luckier than finding a rabbit's foot in a field of clovers. Yamaguchi slept and then boarded a train out of the city the next day to safety.

Yamaguchi arrived in Nagasaki on August 9 and after receiving medical care, reported promptly for work. Yamaguchi's stories of a bomb powerful enough to flatten a city were met with derision from his employees and boss. He was desperately trying to inform his supervisor of the devastation that he had left behind when another bright flash engulfed the sky as a second nuclear bomb was dropped on Yamaguchi's home city.

Yamaguchi spent the next week vomiting, suffering from radiation sickness, but he lived a long life. He married his wife in the early 1950s and had two daughters. He spent much of his life advocating for the disarmament of nuclear weapons and eventually died in 2010 at the ripe old age of 93.

(un)Lucky or what?

HEMINGWAY'S NEW ATLANTIS

Sometimes in history, someone does something that seems so bizarrely stubborn that one almost feels the need to stand up, clap, and then berate oneself for failing to do it first. An example of this is the actions of a man called Leicester (pronounced Lester) Hemingway, the brother of celebrated author Ernest Hemingway. In 1964, Leicester decided that he would establish his own country. Leicester was the founder and, after a vote, the president of the nation of the Republic of New Atlantis. Leicester preceded his bizarre move by telling the *Washington Post*:

"There's no law that says you can't start your own country."

Shortly after this, Leicester founded the new nation of the *Republic of New Atlantis* on July 4 by anchoring an 8x30 foot bamboo raft with a Ford engine. He settled some six miles from the coast of Jamaica, which was recognized as International Waters at the time. He declared the raft and all water and land around him as half being part of the Republic and half belonging to the United States of America. Under the Guano Islands Act of 1856, all Americans were permitted to claim unclaimed islands in the name of America should they possess guano deposits.

Interestingly, by 1965 there was a small population of 12 people that made up *New Atlantis*, mainly Hemingway's family plus his assistant and PR specialist. Hemingway's wife constructed a flag for the micronation, and he was quickly elected President of *New Atlantis* by the entire population in the nation's first-ever democratic election, bringing an end to its dictatorship period.

Hemingway was experimenting with what democracy was as well as donating to marine research in Jamaica. Batches of stamps were designed and eventually mailed to the White House, one showing an image of Lyndon B Johnson. The White House responded to him as

"Acting President" and Hemingway claimed full international recognition, thus legitimized his nation. He made moves to expand the island by piling up rocks underneath as well as claiming the sea 50 feet beneath his raft.

Unfortunately, the nation was destroyed within a few years by a tropical storm, bringing Hemingway's experiments to a premature end. It all sounds so easy to do. Especially as the Guano Islands Act hasn't yet been repealed…, please, no one tell Kanye West.

"1ST PLACE TO MRS. MIGGINS FOR SCREAMING AT BOB!"

The Iowa State Fair is a massive occasion for Iowa. Taking place across 11 days in August every year, it attracts thousands of attendees from inside and outside the state. Some of the events that feature there include agricultural contests to see who has bred the biggest boar, musical guests to entertain the crowd and a cow sculpted from butter. It generally sounds like a great experience for most, though perhaps if you are a husband that wishes to avoid dying from embarrassment, you should consider staying away.

The Iowa State Fair also boasts the Husband Calling Competition, which is precisely what it says on the tin, a spouse - most usually a wife - stands on stage and yells their husband's name at the top of their lungs. Whoever does it the best, wins. The competition came from a time before mobile phones, where wives would yell across a field to let their husbands know that dinner was ready. Finding an exact date for its start is tough, but there's evidence of the competition going back to the 1980s at least.

In 2023, videos of the husband calling went viral, gaining millions of views across the internet as bemused viewers questioned the definitions of sport and competition. The contestants are welcome to do their calling exactly as they wish. Some go for a good old-fashioned yell:

"BOB!!!!! BBOBBBBBB! COME BACK HERE, BOB!"

Whereas some like to take a different tack. That might be yodeling:

"AhodeloDEE-odee-lodee-IAAAAAAN-iedolodieEEEIAAAAAAN"

Or opera singing. Or, in some instances, just straight-up insults, as seen in 2017:

"What am I supposed to call him? You low-down, stinky, manure-covered, farmer-tanned - oh I have to call him for dinner? DAAARYLLLLLL!"

The competition is a bit bizarre. The winners are chosen by a select panel of judges (not sure how they're chosen for the job), but a big factor must be the humor of it. The competition is universally funny. The people competing in it do not hold back, fully launching into their hollering, singing, and trilling all in the name of having a good laugh at the idea of someone actually calling their husband in this way. In 2022, the first male competitor entered, called Jason Clayworth, and he won sixth place. Perhaps from now, we'll see more variety in the screaming at husbands.

I THINK THEY BOUGHT IT...

Many of us don't enjoy our jobs for various reasons. It might be boring, stressful, difficult, poorly paid, or involve atrocious co-workers. Either way, sometimes - though it may shock you - we need a day off from our jobs. There are many legitimate reasons, of course, like a funeral or for health reasons, but sometimes people simply make up a believable enough excuse and deliver it to their boss with the same confidence a postman might deliver a package that he knows he just stamped.

Europeans take an average of 7.3 sick days per year, which makes America and Asia look like they house the most diligent workers ever. Many American and Asian businesses don't offer any paid sick leave, so if you're ill, then you lose out on work, which might explain it. However, the biggest shirkers in the world are those who live in the United Kingdom. UK workers take, on average, 9.1 days off per year for sickness-related reasons. It's a wonder they get anything done over there!

Taking a day off is actually an ancient practice. We have recorded evidence of Ancient Egyptian excuses engraved on a small tablet that offers a fascinating glimpse into how this wonderful society tried to secure a day off. Put yourself into the sandals of an Egyptian boss: perhaps you're looking after construction or running a shop selling food and wares. Respond (out loud or in your head, depending on whether you're on a bus or not) to the excuses for your own amusement.

Penduauu: *I do apologize boss, but I can't work today, I will be drinking with Khonsu on this fine Spring Day. Thanks!*

Sawadjyt: *I know that this is the third day off this year, but you have to understand that my daughter is on her period so I simply must be at home. Cheers.*

Horemwia: *Gosh it's a gorgeous day isn't it boss? Even in winter. Now look, I can't quite come in today as I am at the crucial stage of crafting my home-*

brewed beer. I am quite sure that I've almost cracked the perfect recipe. I'll bring you some next time I'm in!

Aapehti: *I'm certain you wouldn't be upset to learn that I can't come into our place of employ as I must make an offering to the Gods. I'm sure you wouldn't refuse me time off for securing the safety of my mortal soul, would you?*

Paherypedjet: *My scribe needs some stone to write on, I'm going to go and get it for him. As such, I doubt very much that I'll be able to make it into work really. Much obliged.*

It's a wonder that the pyramids were ever completed.

CASTRO AND THE
PAINTED SEASHELL

We've already examined bizarre assassination attempts on Churchill in this book, but his pale in comparison to the CIA's endeavors to bring an early end to Fidel Castro's life.

But why were they so bothered about killing Castro?

Fidel Castro was a Cuban revolutionary who installed communist rule in Cuba in the 1950s. Throughout the 20th century, Cuba and America had very strained relations because of Cuba's communist politics as well as its proximity to the States. In fact, for two weeks in October 1962, the two countries came extremely close to launching nuclear weapons at each other, which could have sparked a war that would have threatened all of humanity. The CIA didn't love Fidel Castro; he was seen as a very dangerous man who possessed a dangerously bushy beard.

So, the CIA and others supposedly launched 634 attempts on Castro's life. There were so many tried and failed that the Cuban leader once said:

"If surviving assassination attempts were an Olympic event, I would win the Gold medal."

Knowing that Castro was a keen diver, the CIA attempted to pack a mollusk with explosives to detonate when Castro was in the vicinity. They also prepared a diving suit for him that was laced with a fungus that would cause a fatal sickness when he put it on. These slightly zanier ideas weren't actually tried but several were attempted, though all failed, as Castro died in 2016 at the age of 90 from natural causes.

The assassination attempts that were carried out include the following:

- A Cuban agent was handed a poison pen equipped with a needle in 1961. He was disappointed in the plan and refused to use it. He asked for something "more sophisticated."
- Marita Lorenz, one of Castro's former lovers, was given poison pills to put in his drink. Castro found out and instead gave her his gun, before laughing at her for trying to kill him and then they proceeded to make love.
- The CIA apparently sought to give Castro an exploding cigar in the 1960s, given his love for the product; however, this either failed or never made its way to Castro in the first place.
- In 2000, Castro was due to speak in Panama when his security detail discovered 198 pounds of explosives hidden under the podium, which would have ensured the speech went off with a bang.

The list of attempts is borderline endless, and some are unlikely to ever be disclosed. Regardless, Castro's knack for snuffing out the danger and removing it is uncanny, almost impressive. Perhaps, if the CIA were to check the coffin to make sure he was definitely dead, they'd be greeted with an empty box and a note saying "Ha! Ha!"

THEY SHALL NOT
GROWL OLD

Why are there so many crazy stories from World War II? Perhaps it's because it was such a crazy time. There were bound to be some quite bonkers little stories happening inside of it. Well, this one comes from 1942 in the ranks of the Polish military, which had joined forces with the Soviet Union to fight Nazi Germany. If you were part of the Polish II Corps, a tactical arm of the Polish armed forces, in 1942, then you may have been introduced to Wojtek, who would be joining your ranks after being bought from an Iranian boy.

Oh, and by the way, Wojtek is a bear.

The Polish II Corps were taking many Polish civilians from the Soviet Union to Iran, where they should be safer when a young girl called Irena saw the bear cub. She approached the Lieutenant and begged him to purchase the bear for her, so she may look after it. Many adults, when asked to buy a ludicrous thing by a child will respond with "No, absolutely not." In this instance, however, it may have been more sensible to say "No, absolutely not, who on earth would purchase a bear for you? I mean come on now, it's a bear, it will probably kill you."

Nevertheless, the bear was purchased and raised by Irena until he was eventually seen as a mascot for the 22nd company and traveled to Iraq, Syria, Palestine, and Egypt (making him better traveled than 85% of American citizens). He was enlisted as a private quickly so that rations could be given to him, which meant he drank beer, ate fruit, and supposedly smoked cigarettes. It was said he even walked up right after he'd seen so many soldiers do so before him.

Wojtek was of crucial use in the Italian Campaign, which the 22nd company fought alongside the British. British regulations said that no mascots or pets were allowed, but this wasn't a problem as Wojtek was, of course, an enlisted soldier and *not* a mascot. During the Battle of Monte Cassino, Wojtek worked hard as a laborer, carting round massive amounts of ammo and proving crucial to the Allied forces' victory. Many English soldiers reported seeing a bear carrying ammo at least once, though were baffled as to why. Wojtek was made Corporal following the skirmish and the 22nd company adopted a symbol of a bear carrying ammunition as their official emblem.

Wojtek was transported to Scotland, along with the rest of the 22nd company, after the war, and he lived out the rest of his life in Edinburgh Zoo. Wojtek responded to commands in Polish and recognized members of his old company and even had many spots on TV. As Corporal, he could boss around soldiers too, but all he ever asked for was "honey, and lots of it."

TELETUBBIES
SAY GO AWAY!

Have you ever seen *Teletubbies*? If not, then here's a brief description.

Teletubbies was a show for very small children, let's say the ages of about two to four. The show is about four creatures called Teletubbies who are humanoid, soft plush creatures that talk in a nonsensical baby speak. They have television screens on their stomachs that occasionally catch broadcasts of 1970s sports (not true, that's a joke) and live in a dome house with a hoover that has managed to achieve autonomy. At the start and end of every episode, a sun that has a baby's face appears over the rolling hills of their pretty landscape and the Teletubbies say "Eh-Oh!"

The whole thing is a nightmare, but kids absolutely loved it and it was popular in many countries. *Teletubbies* no longer runs as a show but still has an appeal for young children and offers harmless viewing. As such, the location of their land has been a popular tourist destination for a long time. The rolling hills were located in Warwickshire, on a small farm, and from the show's inception in 1997 onward, people have flocked to have their picture taken by the famous landmark.

Harmless. Unless you own the land. Rosemary Harding owns the lovely site and in 2013 said:

> *"We were absolutely fed up with people trespassing trying to catch a glimpse of the secluded area - it was never meant to be a tourist attraction. We had people jumping fences, crossing cattle fields and all sorts - it was a nightmare for everyone."*

Rosemary decided, therefore, to flood the area so that no one would be able to visit. She insists that she is far happier now that no *Teletubbies* fans can come to see the old set. Now a family of swans and freshwater fish occupy the area and if you listen closely, you can hear the faint sound of a Teletubby coming home for Tubby Toast. "Eh-Oh!"

I'D TAKE IT OVER
TELEMARKETING

If you're pressed to discuss the worst jobs in the world then many options come to mind: a laborer in a developing country, a minimum wage customer service assistant, or a telemarketer. All are unpleasant jobs at many times and aren't given much credit for how much good they do for society (apart from telemarketers, their job is pointless).

But as difficult or unpleasant as they can be, one can think of very few jobs that are much worse than being a gong farmer.

Heading off any misconception here, the gong farmer has nothing to do with the East Asian percussion instrument "the gong." Gong here means something very different.

In Medieval Europe, most castles operated with a cesspit. A cesspit is basically a big hole where all the human waste is put; it's where all the toilets lead to. This is far more sanitary for the "user" of the toilet, as they don't have to clear out their own business, but it does make the job more unpleasant for someone else. Ultimately, you can put all your waste in a big hole, but what happens when that hole fills up? Well, you call the gong farmer.

They were also known as nightmen and they would come to the castles at night and empty the cesspit and transport the contents away to a prearranged area where it would be buried. Now, the gong farmer is unlikely to come by weekly or maybe not even monthly; cesspits are large, and it takes a long time to fill them. So, the gong farmer may come just once a year in some instances. If you can imagine what that hole must smell like, well then you must have smelt some pretty heinous things in your life.

Gong farmers weren't in any way admired in society; in fact, many looked down on them, which seems cruel. They were paid by the ton of waste removed, so the amount of physical and grotesque labor involved, only to be looked down on, is somewhat heartbreaking.

Still, at least they're not telemarketers.

SERIOUSLY, WHAT IS THE BIG DEAL ABOUT IT?

If you are asked to think of art, then some wonderful paintings may come to mind from superb artists who have drastically altered how human beings communicate and love for centuries. Van Gogh's *Starry Night*, Grant Wood's *American Gothic*, Johannes Vermeer's *Girl With a Pearl Earring*; the list is endless, but the crown for the most recognizable piece has to go to Leonardo Da Vinci. Da Vinci created some spectacular works such as the *Vitruvian Man* and his representation of *The Last Supper*, but ultimately, it is the *Mona Lisa* that is the most recognizable piece of art in the world.

But why?

The *Mona Lisa* is a very good painting, no one would deny this, but there's not too much that makes it stand out. It's a portrait, not particularly big, of a woman (also not particularly big). She's smiling, slightly, but that's it. So why are people so obsessed? Why are there queues out the door at the Louvre in France to see it? Well, the answer lies in a bizarre event that took place in 1911.

On August 21, 1911, the *Mona Lisa* was stolen from the Louvre. Apparently, it took some 28 hours to even notice it was gone initially; it wasn't really considered an important painting up until this point, apart from by some true art aficionados who really liked it for some reason. The theft was only noticed because an artist was supposed to be painting the gallery it hung in, and he noticed it wasn't there. He asked the guards when it was due to be put back in the gallery by the photographers and when the photographers responded that they didn't have it, the alarm was rung. *The New York Times* ran the headline:

60 DETECTIVES SEEK STOLEN 'MONA LISA'

Three Italians had run off with the painting and hoped to quickly sell it, to make a quick buck, especially as rumors of war had been gaining traction. However, they weren't able to; the case was now far too famous, making the purchase of the painting far too dangerous for anyone to consider. Vincenzo Perugia, the mastermind, kept it for 28 months before trying to sell it. The dealer who came to look at it called the police, and it was returned. But for 28 months the world had heard about the tragic loss of the *Mona Lisa* and its eventual, thankful, return.

So next time you see an image of the *Mona Lisa* somewhere, ask yourself: "Would anyone care about it if it hadn't been stolen?"

THE COMPETITIVELY BEARDED DRUG DEALER

Some lives are just so bizarre that you barely know where to start, apart from questioning what on earth you can do to become more interesting. Such is the life and times of Gal Vallerius, otherwise known as Oxymonster, who was arrested back in 2017 on his way to the "2017 Beard and Moustache Championships" in Austin, Texas.

Vallerius had been a competitive beard grower for almost 20 years and was a striking sight with his expertly plucked and preened facial plumage. However, he had a side hustle. To be fair, there's not necessarily tons of money in competitive beard growing, so perhaps that's why he sought out another avenue for earning. Some people become bartenders or perhaps drive Ubers as second jobs, but instead, Vallerius eyed the career of an international drug baron.

Operating under the pseudonym Oxymonster, he trafficked illegal drugs around the world via the Dark Web. The Dark Web is a part of the internet that is without rules and boundaries, with illegal drugs being somewhat easy to attain. Those that use the Dark Web are monitored by governments around the world due to the illegal nature of much activity there, and the federal authorities of America became very interested in the 38-year-old Frenchman's activities.

He has been prosecuted and is now unable to compete in beard-related competitions, nor walk around freely for 20 years.

THIS BITE MIGHT
BE YOUR LAST

"Death by Food," is a not uncommon form of death, but it can refer to many ways of dying that are related to the consumption of grub. Food can be contagious and cause death via bacteria, it could cause anaphylaxis leading to suffocation, or one could simply fail to swallow properly. As Alanis Morrisette would say, "Isn't it ironic" that what we require to keep us alive can kill us. In fact, isn't odd that it doesn't happen more? Some people fail to understand how a circle doesn't fit into a square, yet those same people manage to successfully maneuver a chewed-up ham sandwich around their mouths without somehow choking to death. Here are a few stories that show that our relationship with food isn't often that healthy and often because of our own stupidity.

For instance, the King of Sweden in 1771 consumed an entire feast that could have happily fed dozens of fully grown adults. He inhaled caviar, lobster, and champagne and finished the meal with 14 servings of a traditional pudding called semla. In a scene as equally impressive as grotesque, the King died that same night from digestion problems.

Sherwood Anderson, the novelist who wrote *Whinesburg, Ohio* and *The Triumph of the Egg* (haven't read 'em? Yeah, me, neither!) was felled by a humble snack and in a way that was really not his fault (though perhaps a little his fault). On a cruise with his wife, Anderson complained of stomach cramps and later died of them. It was found that he'd managed to somehow swallow a whole toothpick, thus spearing and damaging his internal organs. This is clearly a case of someone just not paying attention when popping an olive in their mouth. How do you not notice the toothpick? Try it, you'll notice it.

Lastly, a piece of friendly advice: if fugu is offered to you, you should immediately turn it down and briskly walk away shouting, "Get away from me, you psychopath!" Fugu is an infamous Japanese blowfish that gained worldwide attention from *The Simpsons* in the 1990s. The fish has several parts of it that are poisonous and almost certainly fatal if consumed, including the liver. In 1975, Bando Mitsugoro VIII, an actor, announced that he could eat the liver due to his immense power. He ordered the fish liver (illegal to serve, by the way), ate it, and died.

If in doubt, ask yourself, "Will eating this cause some serious complications?" If the answer's yes, then just don't do it. Unless you're a Swedish King; then, you can do what you like.

KEBAB, ANYONE?

The days of populating America with White Americans in the 19th century, under a policy known as Manifest Destiny, were dangerous. Christian Americans were told to go and populate the landmass of America as commanded by God. This led many brave (and occasionally stupid) people to embark on a perilous journey battling mountain ranges, aggressive wildlife, and Native Americans who were none too pleased with the immediate expansion of White territory. Many people lost their lives and lived in extreme isolation and poverty to settle in America. Was it worth it? Sure!

One group has gone down in history as an example of how badly exploration can go if you don't plan your journey very, very carefully. This group are known as The Donner Party.

The Donner Party were a group of 87, made up of different families, who were journeying to California from Illinois in 1846 to capitalize on the newfound wealth in the region. The party set off in May 1846 and just about made every mistake that you could make along the way. The first mistake has already been mentioned, can you spot it? Well, it transpires that to complete a six-month trip across America safely, one should leave sometime before May. You'll find out why in a moment.

The trip went relatively normal at first. The party traveled along the Oregon Trail and made it to Fort Bridger in what is now Wyoming. The group was having problems involving the health of many party members, including children who were suffering from consumption. At Fort Bridger, they received word of what is now called The Hastings Cutoff, a diversion from the well-established Oregon Trail set out by Lansford Hastings. He claimed that his new route, which went by the Great Salt Lake in modern-day Utah, would shave a great deal of time off of their journey. The party was split on the matter and, literally, split over the matter.

The majority journeyed on along the Hastings Cutoff and quickly ran into problems. The terrain was far, far more difficult on the new route and the group were heavily delayed. By August, food was beginning to run out with little sign of help. On August 25, the first party member died, and the group prepared to journey over a 984-foot mountain. From its peak they saw a barren desolate flat covered in salt and were exceptionally demoralized.

The group fell apart, with infighting leading to more splinter groups. Some left the ragtag Donner Party to continue, but many felt that they were too far along to turn around. The group had been heavily delayed and decided to make camp at Truckee Lake, building cabins and basic lodgings.

From November 1846 to March 1847, the group suffered greatly. Many of the group died and some suffered from psychosis and hallucinations, or lost their sanity due to the extreme isolation and feelings that all hope had been lost.

Almost half the group failed to survive the winter and those who fell unfortunately became food for the starving camp. Eventually, the group was rescued. Many of the children had become orphans. There was a great deal of media coverage examining the nightmare endured by the families.

The Donner Kebab was then invented in 1848 - just kidding, the modern *doner* kebab sandwich was invented in the late 20th century. But try to have one now with the extra red sauce without thinking of this story!

"YOU'RE UNDER ARREST FOR POSSESSION OF A GHASTLY HAT"

Have you ever seen an outfit that makes you wish that the person wearing it would be arrested and thrown away forever? An outfit so atrociously bad that it makes you wonder if people should even be allowed to leave their house if they insist on looking like that. Often one looks back on their own fashion history with a grimace: the poor-fitting jeans, the oversized hat, the wearing of a rugby top in a bar. Even historically, the Tudors should have been told that the ruff wasn't going to be a fashion item that would stand the test of time. And most historians agree that Abraham Lincoln would now look back on *that hat* with a sick feeling in his stomach if he could see what a hairdryer and cheap hairspray can do for a man's hairline in the 21st century.

These fashion purveyors, these fashion police, unfortunately, don't exist and thus faddish mistakes are made every day that deserves a lengthy community service sentence. But for a brief moment in time in Augusta, Georgia, there was an active taskforce that would stop one from making the biggest of fashion *faux pas*: wearing a straw hat.

The date is somewhere in mid-September 1918. If you turned to your *Augusta Chronicle* on this day (hopefully it was delivered okay), then you'd have seen an article declaring:

"*Straw Hats are doomed for the season.*"

"BLAST!" You think to yourself. You'd just bought 19 of them; if only someone had told you! From this time on, however, if you were spotted with a straw hat on, then anyone would be permitted to grab that garment from your head and, with great conviction, stamp on it so it resembled a shredded wheat frisbee.

In general, it was seen that the summer months were acceptable straw hat-wearing days; they were permissible and even encouraged at times. But once the summer drew to a close, it was felt that the headwear should be abandoned like a grassy Wilson from *Cast Away*, though ideally with less crying.

In some rare instances, violence erupted in response to the forced decrees on wearing this normally inoffensive and simple item. In 1922, New York City contended with the Straw Hat Riot, seeing mass hysteria, fighting, and generalized disorder across the city.

Maybe you should consider this next time you decide to wear an oversized Hawaiian shirt to the theater...

LISTERINE OR LISTURINE?

Do you use mouthwash? Well, you should. Nine out of ten dentists agree that those who use mouthwash have healthier mouths. However, nine out of ten dentists seemingly agree on everything. The last dentist is just very surly. Craig, he's called, and he's not a pleasant man; do not attempt to get him to agree to anything.

Mouthwash was invented in late 1879 by Dr. Lawrence for the company Johnson & Johnson. It was an effective bacteria killer, used for cleaning up your gob-hole and for sterilizing wounds. It was named after Joseph Lister, who was also largely responsible for coming up with the novel idea of "cleaning all surgical tools and areas before you cut into someone's body" in 1865. The mortality rates in Lister's patients plummeted and doctors began sanitizing in clinical settings.

Prior to the Victorian-era doctors making genuinely impressive leaps in mouthwash technology, in the 18th century, Anton van Leeuwenhoek had discovered that bacteria existed. He began knocking back alcohol to destroy the little germs and it became a popular method of washing out one's mouth. This was partially because it's effective and partially because it gets you a bit drunk first thing in the morning. Alcohol is still in fact present in many mouthwashes today; just make sure you're not knocking back a bottle a day.

Through the medieval era, little care was paid to teeth health. They have gone a bit brown and sometimes a tooth had to be removed, but people generally weren't living long enough to see the long-term effects of poor dental hygiene…, or they just didn't care. Tortoise blood became a popular disinfectant (this doesn't work) as well as herbal concoctions of berries, mint, vinegar, and wine (this weirdly doesn't work either).

If we trace mouthwash back further to the Ancient Romans and the earliest recorded signs of mouthwash, the most revolting effort is found. The Romans used to swill urine imported from Portugal, thinking that it was helping somehow (please acknowledge that it doesn't, even if it's just to yourself). Urine was a cheap and common mouthwash well into the 18th century, but what's truly interesting is that it was presumably many people's jobs to urinate into pots and then sell it to the Romans for a mighty profit. Many of us wish for that level of job security in the 21st century.

THE TOXIC LADY

This story is more peculiar, unfortunate, and baffling than it is funny. But it's one worth knowing and considering over the next few days. Cast your mind back *all the way* to 1994.

A woman by the name of Gloria Ramirez has just been rushed to hospital. She is unfortunately sick with cancer and had just taken a turn for the worst, with a drop in blood pressure and struggling with forming sentences. Doctors get to work but nothing is working. The nurses remove her shirt and notice that Ramirez's skin looks a bit strange, almost shiny. A blood sample is taken. All seems wrong, with a foreign substance being present.

Suddenly, a nurse faints and many others begin to experience severe breathing problems. One nurse has even collapsed, suffering from paralysis. A general evacuation is ordered of all emergency departments, and in the end, 23 people are taken ill with five being in a serious enough condition to require hospitalization. But why? The doctors continue with many different techniques and attempts to save Ramirez's life, but regretfully, she died that night. She was then examined by different doctors and experts, with three autopsies taking place.

The autopsies all concluded that she'd died from heart failure, related to earlier kidney failure, all exacerbated by her underlying condition. But no one could quite work out what had caused several professional health practitioners to collapse, lose breath, or even temporarily lose full body function. Ramirez was dubbed The Toxic Lady as people didn't quite seem able to get near her without becoming ill. That was perhaps a touch insensitive but the whole thing was very strange.

Some theories are that she had been using powerful domestic cleaning products as a form of pain management, which may have introduced some unsafe chemicals into her system. However, there hasn't been a confirmed reason yet, and the case remains a mystery.

GENERAL SEDGWICK'S
FAMOUS LAST WORDS

People's last words is a highly interesting topic that make for great quiz rounds and small talk if you're struggling with the in-laws. Many people carefully consider what they want their last words to be. Perhaps if you're extremely careful, you could deliver a prediction, as Nostradamus did in 1566.

"Tomorrow, at sunrise, I shall no longer be here."

You could show a sense of dignity and poise as Marie Antoinette managed to before her execution in 1793. She accidentally trod on the foot of her executer, turned to him, and simply said:

"Pardonnez-moi, monsieur (Excuse me, sir)."

Of course, you could just be funny like Buddy Rich, acclaimed jazz drummer, who upon his deathbed in 1987 was asked, "Is there anything you can't take?"

"Yeah, country music."

In reality, of course, many of the famous last words that we're told aren't really last words; they're simply the last *recorded* words that were said. Most likely they've been deliberately chosen for their pithiness, humor, and brevity. If someone is lucky enough to have a deathbed, so to speak, in those few last moments with family and doctors, they are often discussing their estate, answering doctor's questions, or maybe even telling off their kids. "Shut up, Billy," just aren't great last words.

However, someone who truly did have remarkable last words was General John Sedgwick, who died in 1864 toward the back end of the American Civil War.

Sedgwick was part of the Union Army and saw a great deal of action throughout the conflict, becoming a trusted general and leader. His final battle was The Battle of Spotsylvania Court House in May 1864, where his brigade was under heavy fire at the hands of the Confederate soldiers. Bullets were zipping through the sky above Sedgwick's soldiers' heads as they cowered away, absolutely terrified. Sedgwick decided that he needed to inspire the troops and show them that there was no reason to be so afraid - the war had to be won after all and to do so, you need confident troops! He stood up confidently, turned to his soldiers, and asked:

"Why are you dodging like this? They couldn't hit an elephant at this distance."

General Sedgwick was then shot in the head by a Confederate sharpshooter and died, making him the highest-ranking Union death in the war. It would be a shame if it wasn't really quite funny.

YOU PICKED THE WRONG HOUSE! NOW SIT DOWN AND EAT

What does your grandmother do? Or what *did* she do (if yours is sadly not with us any longer)? The top five stereotypical things that grandmothers do are:

1. Bake things
2. Feed anyone who walks into the house
3. Nap
4. Fail to understand anything made by Apple
5. Make sure that tissues are constantly at hand.

If these all seem correct, ask yourself whether your grandmother has ever taken up bodybuilding after she retired. Probably not, but an amazing woman by the name of Willie Murphy from Rochester, New York did exactly that. Willie took up bodybuilding in her older years and currently holds several state weightlifting records in the over-70s categories. She laments the lack of elderly bodybuilders whom she can work out with and encourages the retired to give it a go.

Willie gained a massive amount of attention in 2019, at the age of 82 when a man came up with the wonderfully smart idea of being beaten up by a grandma. Or rather, he tried to rob Willie.

CNN reported that a man forcefully gained access to Willie's home after she refused to open the door to him, despite him pretending to be in distress. As the man kicked her door down, Willie decided to start on him with a table that was to hand and managed to break the household item on the man's body. She grabbed the metal legs from the table and kept hitting the intruder, further incapacitating him. She jumped on him before squirting baby shampoo into his face as he attempted to regain some composure and dignity. She picked up a broom and lay into him a few times further before he'd clearly had enough of the ol' can-o-whoop-ass.

Willie continues to body build and, as of her mid-80s, was able to deadlift 225 pounds. When your parents retire, keep an eye on their hobbies. If they consider picking up a jigsaw, why not suggest that they take out a subscription to a 24-hour gym for their own safety - and plenty of likes on Instagram?

YOU'LL HAVE TO COME IN,
I'M ON THE LAVATORY

They say that you can calm your nerves at a job interview or public speaking event by imagining the audience naked. This can work wonders unless you get completely distracted and lose your train of thought.

Though the trick is as old as the jar of jam that's in your grandma's fridge, another less well-known method is to take a meeting or call while you are relieving yourself in the lavatory. It's likely that since the COVID-19 pandemic, toilet-based functionality has increased by some 750% as people pretend to be intrigued in a meeting and mute themselves while *dropping the kids off at the pool*, as it were. Famously, Lyndon B Johnson, President of the United States from 1963–69 was a fan of taking important meetings while he had parked himself on his porcelain throne.

According to the biography on LBJ produced by historian Robert Dallek, Johnson would abuse his aides with humiliating shouting and insults, before hauling them in for a dressing down in the bathroom. Apparently, the members of staff got used to it quickly, as bizarre as it was. The psychology behind the liaisons is thought to be down to the unconventional power dynamics at play. In the company of someone relieving themselves, you're not the one in control. Perhaps a new saying should be devised based on this:

"They who make the biggest stink, are the last to blink."

There we go, use that at your leisure.

Other famous managers have used the old bathroom technique, such as Sir Alex Ferguson, former manager of Manchester United Football Club, who would routinely conduct business while relieving himself - and he's the most successful soccer coach of all time!

134

Perhaps it's worth trying the next time you have some important work to do. Just pull down your trousers and relieve the pressure in two different ways. Unless you're a welder.

TURKEYS: THE OG BALD EAGLE

The bald eagle is strongly associated with the United States of America. The great predator of the sky, with its white head and black body, has a pointed, dagger-like, yellow beak and penetrative eyes that it uses to search for any prey. It's a symbol of pride and bravery, proudly dominating the United States' Great Seal, its official symbol.

However, when it comes to this historic image, there is a story that repeatedly and apologetically staggers through the mist of unconfirmed history like a husband who swore he'd be home four hours ago. It's the story of Benjamin Franklin attempting to make the national bird of the United States of America a turkey!

Ultimately, the story is a mis-telling of a letter that Franklin sent to his daughter. Upon seeing the design for the bald eagle Great Seal, he wrote that the bird looked more like a turkey than a bald eagle, now so synonymous with power, prosperity, and freedom as it is. Interestingly, Franklin went on to complain that the bald eagle is "dishonest" because the eagle is "too lazy to fish for himself." In Franklin's eye, the national bird should represent what an American should be: self-preserving, innovative, and brave.

He does later go on to suggest in the letter that the turkey would be a *better* bird:

> "… [the turkey] is a much more respectable bird, and withal a true original Native of America…He is, though a little vain & silly, a bird of Courage."

So, Benjamin Franklin didn't quite suggest that a turkey should be the national bird, he just said that it would be *better* than a bald eagle. Who knows what he would have chosen if it were up to him? Perhaps an emu or a small chicken?

WHICH ONE OF YOU TAUGHT HIM TO SAY THAT?

What reason is there to own a parrot other than to hear it say things as it mimics human language? If that's the only purpose, then it's a noble and superbly worthwhile one. People like to hear "I love you," because they're inherently lonely, or perhaps a more pirate-y "pieces of eight," if you like. If you search for "singing parrot" on YouTube, then you're undoubtedly going to be impressed by feathered covers of hit pop songs of the 21st century in a manner only slightly less squawky than the original artist recorded.

However, as a zoo found out in 2020, sometimes parrots can be taught a few *other* things, outside of "Polly wants a cracker."

Staff at the Lincolnshire Wildlife Centre were aghast when they discovered that five African gray parrots who had joined in August of that year were swearing profusely at guests. The fearsome five were named Billy, Eric, Tyson, Jade, and Elsie. This almost impossibly crude gang had to be moved away from to prevent interactions with the public following complaints.

The chief executive of the Centre, Steve Nichols, admitted that it's not uncommon for parrots to pick up on swearing. But normally, when confronted with a passing stream of gawping spectators, they are too nervous to say anything. However, the five aforementioned "fowl"-mouthed birds seemed to relish the attention.

Ultimately, parrots learn to say something to humans because of the reaction that humans give them. Either with praise or food, they learn that humans like to hear a certain sound, so they learn to say it to interact with their compatriots. The birds realized that if they dropped an "f" here, an "s" there, or even the occasional "m," "j," "z," "d," or "w", then people would laugh and smile at the parrot. The worry for the zoo is what to do if the other 200 birds in the parrot colony pick up on the bad habit. I guess they'd just have to lean into it:

COME TO LINCOLNSHIRE WILDLIFE CENTRE

Home to the wonderful band of swearing parrots. Bring your grandma and watch her faint as the parrot tells her what you won't!

INKY THE ESCAPE ARTIST

The great escape artists of our time are rightly revered, being able to effortlessly remove themselves from their chains to taste that sweet nectar of freedom that the rest of us enjoy so readily.

One thinks of Harry Houdini, the magician who could escape any trap that he was put in. He'd be chained up, in an enclosed tank, underwater, and he'd always manage to wriggle out of it in some impossible way.

David Blaine was amazing in the 21st century by being both an escape artist as well as sitting in a case, hanging above the River Thames, for 44 days.

Christopher Daniel Gay (AKA "Little Houdini"), escaped from the same prison three times in the 1970s, twice to visit his dying parents before handing himself back to police, and the third time to run for his life.

In 2016, a notorious escape artist gained international attention in New Zealand. Viewers were shocked, people gasped, but mostly everyone giggled and said "Aww." His name was Inky, and he is still on the run today – or rather, the *slither* – today.

Inky is an octopus that since 2014 had been housed at the National Aquarium in New Zealand. Proving a popular exhibit (obviously, he's an octopus and they look like aliens; they're always popular), he had achieved a bit of fame already from simply being in the aquarium, but he'd had enough come April 2016.

Staff arrived to work and discovered that Inky wasn't in his usual spot, his tank. The lid of his tank was *slightly* ajar, and a diligent employee noticed a trail of wet spots leading to a drainpipe, the ending of which was in the Pacific Ocean. Inky is likely now enjoying his life...doing whatever octopuses do, in the Pacific Ocean. And all you can say is, "Well done, old chap."

THE GREAT U-BEND
THAT FOUGHT THE NAZIS

The submarines employed by Adolf Hitler during WW2 were the scourge of the Allied forces. They were highly effective and difficult to effectively challenge, and their work almost saw starvation brought to the people of Britain mid-way through the war.

The U-1206 was one such submarine. Launched in 1943, it was a top-of-the-range piece of high-tech naval destruction. Most impressively, it was one of several new submarines that had been kitted out with high-tech toilets. You may think "Really now, how high-tech can a toilet be?" Well, if you're planning on expelling waste while you're 657 feet underneath the surface of the ocean, you need a pretty careful procedure in place to throw it away that doesn't involve any water getting in.

On April 14, 1945, World War II was approximately three weeks away from ending in Europe, and the U-1206 was patrolling near Scotland. The submarine was operating at a depth of 200 feet below sea level and all was going well – until the Commander was informed that something was going completely and utterly wrong on board. A sailor had gone to the lavatory and had attempted to flush the toilet. As such, the vessel was now rapidly filling with water, and they would all be dead shortly unless drastic action was taken!

The high-tech toilet was indeed high-tech, but because it was so high-tech the average sailor shouldn't have been touching it. The skilled engineers on board were all trained in how to properly operate the lavvy and only they were cleared to touch any part of it. Clearly, the unfortunate sailor didn't get the message and may very well have been hit by his own homemade torpedo after gallons of high-pressure water flooded in through the now-broken toilet.

The sub had to surface, fast. In doing so, it was spotted by Allied forces and bombed while in the ocean, before surrendering. By the end of the proceedings, 46 people were captured as Prisoners of War and three died in the calamitous incident.

This leads us to the old submarine song to help you remember: *"If it's yellow, let it mellow, if it's brown…, then go and ask for help."*

THAT'LL SHOW
THOSE PESKY EDITORS

A great writer will do anything for their vision to be realized. In modern times, that may involve answering tedious e-mails for about six months, as minute details are changed and edits are made to the tiniest words of the smallest sentences. Or, of course, one can just self-publish on Amazon and literally no one checks what you've written, giving you total creative freedom and an awful book.

Edith Allonby was a writer in the early 20th century who felt the pain of having to re-write and revise her work. She was a highly regarded schoolteacher in England as well as having one book published in 1903 and a further two in 1905.

Allonby's first two books were set on a fictional planet of her own design and were reviewed as being both fantastical and entertaining. Though gaining some critical acclaim for her work, Allonby was becoming intensely frustrated in her ongoing battle with editors to get the books seen. She felt that their meddling was impairing the quality of her novels and preventing consumers from reading her words.

So, in 1905, as she was putting together her last book, *The Fulfillment*, she came up with an ingenious solution to working with editors and gain publicity to drive up sales. She would kill herself!

Allonby bought carbolic acid, took it, and died at the age of 29. Her suicide note was published across the world and *The Fulfillment* was published exactly as she'd left it…, along with some minor editing and annotations carried out on her behalf (it's what she would have wanted!).

In its inglorious way, her suicide worked. This book was by far the most successful of the three and sales of the previous novels also rose. However, one struggles to advocate this as a genuinely positive way of achieving long-term success.

DID YOU VOTE FOR HIM?
DID ANYONE?

When the United States of America became independent, it was partly a move to eschew the British monarchy and its empire. They were institutions that the American people didn't need, viewed as overly stuffy and rooted in an outdated mode of practice, not in tune with American democracy. So therefore, one has to ask why America had an Emperor from 1859–1880 that was very much allowed to act in pretty much any way that he saw fit. In doing so, this short story will posit that *Emperor Norton*, in many ways, lived one of the best lives *ever*.

Joshua Norton was born in England and lived for many years in Cape Town, South Africa. He left in the 1840s to travel to America and eventually came to San Francisco in 1849. Norton garnered success relatively quickly with a good bout of real estate speculation and trading, though managed to lose most of his money when he tried to corner the rice market. You know, the market that is concerned with one of the world's most bountiful crops. He lost a great deal of money and his reputation in San Francisco was dramatically reduced. Norton was no longer the prosperous and charming businessman that he once was.

Norton became frustrated with the political system of the United States. He's lost his legal battle with the suppliers of the rice he was buying and felt that he'd been let down by the system. So, in July 1859, he wrote out a manifesto that was published in the *San Francisco Daily Evening Bulletin*. It spoke of the need for change and what Norton saw as the major problems in the union.

Two months later, he wrote a letter that reads thusly:

"*At the request and desire of a large majority of the citizens of these United States, I, Joshua Norton declare and proclaim myself Emperor of these United States... I do hereby direct the representatives of the*

different States to assemble in Musical Hall, of this city, on the 1st day
of February next, then and there to make alterations in the existing laws
of the Union as may ameliorate the evils under which the country is
laboring, and thereby cause confidence to exist, both at home and
abroad....

– NORTON I., Emperor of the United States."

Norton had proclaimed himself Emperor! The *Bulletin* decided to print
it as a joke and Norton's reign began.

For the next 21 years, Norton was largely able to do whatever he
wanted within San Francisco. People enjoyed his eccentricity and the
strange pomp offered by having *an Emperor* in their state (even if the
title meant nothing). Norton would parade the streets, inspecting
parks and being seen at important gatherings or events. He wore an
elaborate uniform of blue and gold, with a peacock hat, and held an
ornate walking stick.

A policeman attempted to intern Norton to an asylum for a mental
disorder, but the citizens of San Francisco were outraged, and the
newspaper *Daily Alta* leaped to his defense. Norton had not hurt
anyone, and his actions were broadly charming, so no one desired to
see him imprisoned or "fixed" in any way. He never went to the
asylum, and he received an official apology from the Police Chief.
Norton went on to offer a royal pardon to the policeman that arrested
him, and from that day forth, was saluted by the officers of San
Francisco as he walked past.

Norton went on like this for 21 years. He drank at bars for free, ate
meals for free, and kept company with wealthy and important men.
Remember that he did this because he *said* that he should be able to,
and no one stopped him.

The old con-artist trick is to just act confident enough, and people will
let you get away with anything. They'll even let you be the emperor of
the United States!

WHY AVOID A CURRY
BEFORE THE BIG GAME

Soccer, or "football," is the most watched sport worldwide. Millions of people tune in every week to watch exceptionally well-paid men and women (though if we're being honest, it's mainly the men who are well-paid) kick an old bit of leather around a small field. The footballers themselves are some of the most revered sportspeople on the planet, with some holding online followings large enough to be considered a decently-sized Northern European city, or a small suburb in China. Children dream of being world-famous footballers, with every kick, head, or dribble analyzed and applauded by more people than you could even imagine.

So, to be an elite footballer means a privileged life, but to be one who plays at the prestigious World Cup is about as amazing as it can get. In 1990, the World Cup was hosted in Italy, and it remains to this day as one of the most watched events in history with a television set being tuned in to watch measuring 26 billion times. The opening games had started in the summer and jubilation was rife in England as the nation tuned in to watch a talented squad and dream of what heights they might reach.

England was playing Ireland, and all was going relatively…, normally. The ball went up one end of the pitch and then back down again, then did it again. Eyes were on Gary Lineker, a remarkably successful and talented English striker who had been on fire in the world of soccer for years. Hopes were high that he may provide some brilliance against historical rivals. Gary wasn't feeling superb that day, however. For whatever reason, his belly just wasn't feeling right. In his own words, "I had a bit of a dickie stomach." Not wanting to abandon his teammates, however, he kept it to himself and played in the game.

Toward the end of the first half, Lineker stretched to reach the ball bouncing near him and hit the grass. As he did so, several muscles relaxed in the striker's body and, most notably, a crucial circular muscle around the posterior. Mr. Lineker became immediately conscious of three things: 1) millions and millions and millions of people were watching this game, 2) he had just, on live TV, pooed himself; and 3) millions and millions and millions of people would go on to watch this even after the World Cup had ended for decades to come!

Lineker's teammate rushed over to check he was okay, and the esteemed gentlemen simply looked up and said, "I've s*** myself." What do you do in this situation? Well, Sir (he is an OBE, so his official title is actually Sir) Lineker sort of shuffled his accident out of his shorts, stood up, wiped his hand on the grass and saw out the rest of the half…, and the television cameras caught it all.

Gary Lineker finds it funny to this day and very much has an attitude of "What can you do?" Just remember, avoid a vindaloo before a big game, and if you can't, then make sure you've got brown shorts on.

IF THEY FIND OUT, THEY'LL ERECT STATUES IN MY HONOR

In the modern age, cheating sportspeople are given a rough time of it. Most famously, in 2013, Lance Armstrong, the superstar cyclist who won seven Tour de France titles, publicly admitted to using performance-enhancing drugs to advance his career. He was given a lifetime ban and his titles were removed by the US Anti-Doping Agency and his Olympic bronze medal won in 2000 was revoked. The whole debacle was very public and if you mention the name Lance Armstrong now, people will still tut and say, "what an idiot."

If we look back to Ancient Greece, cheaters were dealt with in a very different manner. If you were caught cheating in any way in Olympia, the site of the Ancient Olympic Games, then you would literally have a statue erected with your name on it. The statues were called "Zanes," large bronze statues of Zeus that would be boldly displayed to the ancient crowds.

The statues were funded almost exclusively by the fines that the judges imposed on the given cheater; the greater the fine, the grander the statue would be. The statues were crafted by the greatest artists of the day and had inscriptions with the offender's name, crime, and fine on them. These were so public to make it clear that the Olympics were for great athletes and not for cheats or those who sought to discredit the great competition. Only 16 pedestals remain of the Zanes, with no full statues, which have either fallen or been stolen as the centuries have passed by.

A few notable cheats are Eupolos, who was fined for bribing three opponents in Boxing, while Kallipos, a wrestler, is the subject of six statues after also being caught out for bribery (must have been quite a lot of bribery). Most unfair though, is the Zane erected for Sarapion who was fined for cowardice. He fled the grounds on the eve of the Olympic Games after becoming nervous about the crowds. Seems a touch harsh to fine someone for being a bit nervous! The equivalent would be a not-quite-bride placing a plaque above her bed in honor of her ex-fiancée who cruelly jilted her at the altar.

THE SALEM TOMATO TRIALS

It was not a great time to be a tomato in 1820 (mind you, feel free to argue that there was ever a great time to be a tomato). The humble fruit (not a vegetable, even though it goes on a salad) had an atrocious reputation in the early 19th century, which is hard to imagine given how commonplace they are in the 21st century. Today, many common recipes involve tomatoes in one form or another, and the world's favorite accompaniment to French fries remains tomato ketchup. But in the 1800s, the tomato was associated with danger and poisoning. This is probably because many pewter plates of the time had small amounts of lead in them and the acid from the tomato activated that. The human eats the tomato, so eats some lead, and so receives a bout of poisoning.

However, a man by the name of Colonel Robert Gibbon Johnson was absolutely fed up with the slanderous reputation that the small red blob had received. He worked as an experienced farmer and horticulturalist, so decided to give the tomato the good name it deserved – it had gained the nickname of *the poison apple*, for goodness' sake! Johnson staged the Salem Tomato Trial on September 25, 1820, in an attempt to bring justice for the harmless thing (also to make sure that pizza would become commonly available worldwide by the 2000s).

Johnson stood outside of the Salem courthouse, a place that had seen such injustice in the past (go and Google "Salem Witch Trials" for more information on this) with a basket of tomatoes. A crowd of 2,000 gathered to watch, keen-eyed, with their hearts in their mouths and their palms sweaty, knees weak, mom's tomato. He briefly spoke about the history of the tomato and why it deserves a new life of innocence. The people listened to the impressive figure before he reached down to select his first victim.

Johnson slowly brought the tomato to his lips and took a bite. Reportedly a woman screamed and fainted at this point, but no one

149

cared; they were all transfixed by the man who'd just ingested a stomach full of vile tomato. He took a further bite, then another, one more still until he'd eaten the whole tomato! He stood there, seemingly fine before raising his arms into the air.

"He's still alive!"

The crowd erupted into laughter and cheering. Music played as Johnson stood outside the courthouse, munching on many more of the tomatoes without vomiting, crying, being in pain, or indeed dying. Thus, the tomato was saved, and we can all enjoy Heinz products without fear of death…, well, not immediately, anyway.

A TSUNAMI OF MOLASSES

Molasses is a useful substance, derived from refining sugarcane, forming a sticky brown liquid. It's used predominantly for brown sugar production, an ingredient in the distilling of various forms of alcohol, and can also be used in munitions manufacturing. All in all, it's a seriously useful and seriously profitable thing to create. But on January 15, 1919, during a strangely warm mid-January day, a bizarre and destructive disaster struck Boston at approximately 12:30 p.m., and it was all because of the sticky gloop that is molasses.

The Purity Distilling Company had stored a large quantity of molasses in a harborside tank, for ease of transporting the molasses via boat to its ethanol plant in Cambridge, Massachusetts. The tank was 49 feet tall, 88 feet in diameter, and contained some 2m gallons of molasses. Some of the molasses had recently been warmed for transportation and had then been placed inside the tank alongside older, colder molasses. The thermal reaction inside the tank created a large amount of pressure and in the middle of the day, the tank burst.

With reports of the ground shaking, exceptionally loud noises of bangs, crashing and crunching metal emanating from the Distilling Company, the citizens of Boston had every reason to be fearful.

The molasses moved with great speed through the streets of downtown Boston, traveling at 35mph, creating a 26-foot-high wave. The sticky goo quickly enveloped anything it came into contact with, causing massive amounts of destruction en route. Several buildings collapsed as their foundations were unable to take the massive amount of energy generated by the wave. Witnesses reported that they saw dozens of horses and other animals get overwhelmed, becoming almost invisible the moment the wave hit.

Unfortunately, the same was true for many Boston citizens. Fighting one's way out of the two to three-foot-deep pool of molasses that had formed was borderline impossible and approximately 150 people were injured or partially drowned by the force of the wave, while 21 people succumbed to the flood and died drowning in the molasses.

The rescue attempt took days. Firefighters, soldiers, and nurses had to wade through the thick goo, and it had become difficult to recognize where there were bodies. Some people had been taken out to the harbor after being hit by the tsunami of molasses and weren't found until several months had passed. Boston itself slowly recovered from the traumatic event, with the clean-up taking some weeks. It was a good year before all signs of the molasses finally disappeared.

The company was sued for their poor storage of the product, and they paid out approximately $100,000 in modern terms for each victim of the flood. They never stored molasses in the same way again. The site of the tragedy is honored with a plaque to this day and remains an important part of Massachusetts' modern history. Maybe think about this story and the manslaughter of 21 Bostonites next time you have a Spiced Rum & Coke out at a bar.

HEN-NEIGH THE HOOVER!

Consider the miracle of a clean floor for just a moment. Every year humans shed tons of dead skin, which helps form the majority of what makes up common household dust and it gets *everywhere* (sorry to make you paranoid about your dirty home). Our countertops, our coffee tables, our wooden floors, and especially our rugs become the home to huge quantities of dust, and we work tirelessly to get rid of it. Or rather, our vacuum cleaners work tirelessly.

The common household vacuum cleaner, or hoover if you like, is one of the staple household goods after the microwave and whisky decanter (right?). Much of the reason for this is that the vacuum is unique in what it does. Some can live without a microwave, and some can exist without needing a kettle, but have you ever seen someone try to extract dust from a carpet without a hoover? Hopefully not, it's disgusting and inefficient.

The beginnings of This helpful device can be spotted in 1901 after an engineer by the name of Hubert Cecil Booth considered a machine that filtered away dust and so, within a few years he designed the first of its kind, the first vacuum called "The Puffing Billy." It was a colossal brightly-colored machine that had to be drawn along by horses (who did their very best to not poo where the machine had hoovered). Seems inconvenient, yes, but it was a roaring success.

Booth was commissioned to clean Crystal Palace in London, for which he had to use 15 Puffing Billys. It took a very dry and dirty month to it pull off. By the end of the job, he'd managed to extract 26 tons of dirt and dust, which presumably led every visitor to Crystal Palace to feel a bit sick.

It didn't take too long for someone to decide that having to own horses to own a vacuum cleaner wasn't convenient for most of the population and William Hoover's company helped create the basic prototype for the machine we use today. But all praise goes to Booth and his horses for their hard work in the first place! A round of applause is required! *Clop Bostonese clop.*

I WONDER IF I'M MISSING SOMETHING OBVIOUS?

You know how we all roller skate now? No? Well, some people do, anyway. It's a fun hobby whereby the skater operates a pair of boots with wheels on them. They do some zooming about, a few turns here and there, before settling back down and having a cup of coffee at home.

Though they seem like a relatively modern, almost faddish invention, roller skates were actually first invented in the 1760s by a man with the spectacular name of John Joseph Merlin. Merlin was attending a rather fancy party event and thought to debut his brand-new fashion item. He decided to pop on his zany new footwear and scoot around the room while playing the violin for the amused and shocked guests. Joseph Merlin was well known for being a fantastic musician and inventor, so this sort of performance was not necessarily uncommon. The crowd laughed, pointed, and cheered for Merlin as he glided around on the novel shoes – what a lark!

The only issue was that Merlin was quite a poor skater. Though, to be fair, he was probably also the best skater in the world at that point. Even still, a flurry of panic must have crept across his face as he realized:

"How do I stop?"

Merlin lost control of his speed quite suddenly, and he careered off through the crowd with no way of stopping – he hadn't put brakes on the skates! He crashed into a huge mirror, which as well as causing him seven years of bad luck, landed him with a massive bill that would make even the Emir of Qatar wince.

Merlin was left with some serious injuries, a destroyed violin, and the need to go back to the drawing board (though he probably just walked to it).

YOU'VE SNEEZED
YOUR LAST

Being the Pope is really quite hard work and especially so in the 17th century when most of the people that the Pope was in charge of weren't able to read. Consequently, back then their job mostly entailed giving simple orders that could be obeyed across the enormous stretch of the Catholic Church, such as "Go to church on Sundays", "Do _____ to avoid illness," or "Give me money, all the money." Things have moved on now as the church has changed over the last two centuries and communication has become easier, but in 1642, Pope Urban VIII attempted to police the impossible.

Pope Urban declared that sneezing was sinful and akin to *sexual ecstasy*. Most people would agree that a sneeze has a certain satisfaction to it, but it may be a bit of a stretch to deem it ecstasy in any form. So, why did he come out with such a bizarre claim?

Well, Pope Urban was an interesting fellow and really rather self-absorbed. He was Pope during the time of the Thirty Years' War and was crucial to updating Italian defense systems, helping to ward off invasion and aggression around Rome. He's best known, though, for his love of opulence and nepotism. That means he was happy to spend lots of money on himself and give great jobs to his family and friends.

The sneezing thing all comes down to a product called "snuff" that was enjoyed across Europe at the time by the rich and powerful. Snuff is a tobacco powder that is inhaled via the nose to give the user an uplifting feeling and to satisfy their urge for nicotine. It also, of course, causes sneezing because things aren't meant to go up your nose and your nose will try to eject all via a good "ahchoo!"

The Pope didn't like snuff, nor indeed any form of tobacco, so he banned it in 1642. He thought the product was sinful and, of course, it led to the unbearably sexual sneeze as mentioned above, so he threatened anyone who didn't follow with ex-communication (banishment from the church). Why in particular he hated snuff is still a bit of a mystery, but a report from Naples claimed that he hated it so much because he took it once and sneezed so hard that he vomited. Perhaps it was all a pride thing. Or perhaps sneezing is indeed devilish and should be avoided at all costs.

SHOULD WE TELL HIM?

If you go to the East End of London, specifically around the Charlton area, and ask many of the older people who Samuel Bartram is then you'll get some appreciative smiles, a few *oohs*, and quite a few responses like, "Who's that? Who are you? Are you, my grandson?"

Bartram actually holds the record for the most appearances for Charlton Athletic, the soccer club where he spent his whole professional career, from 1934 to 1956. He won cups and accolades during his career and remains a beloved figure in the East End to this day, but he's also well known for making himself look like a bit of a fool in front of a whole stadium…, which was empty.

Charlton Athletic was facing Chelsea in 1937, a hot ticket match, it being a London derby after all. The atmosphere was thick with shouting, clapping, and fog. Lots of fog. The fog rolled in from the opposite end to Bartram's after kick-off. The referee called a halt to proceedings as the fog became denser, but then it cleared slightly and the game resumed. Yet the fog still acted as a thick curtain, obscuring Bartram's vision. And oh yeah, Bartram was the goalkeeper.

The game continued and Bartram lost sight of his teammates completely as they attacked the opposite end. Bartram remained poised; at any moment a football would likely be struck toward him, and he would need to pull off a feat of goalkeeping brilliance to keep it out when his view was so obscured. Like a cobra spying on a mouse, he prepared his body for the right time to strike.

Five minutes passed, no shot yet.

Ten minutes now, not a sign.

Fifteen minutes done…then…a figure! A man was approaching the goal…*sloowwwly.*

It was a policeman, who was patrolling the ground to make sure no one had been left in the stadium. Shocked to have discovered a *player* on the pitch, he promptly said to Bartram:

"What on earth are you doing here? The game was stopped a quarter of an hour ago. The field's completely empty."

Bartram fumbled his way to the dressing room where he found his teammates, fully dressed in their civilian clothing, howling with laughter at his misfortune. Bartram saw the very, very funny side and wrote about it in his autobiography some years later. The story goes down as a top tale to tell from English soccer.

IS IT A BIRD? IS IT A PLANE? NO! IT'S A MONK!

Very little is known about Benedictine monks from the 11th century, partly because no one wrote anything down and partly because there's not much to talk about. I'd have 11th-century monks at number three on my "Worst People to Have at a Party." Number two is occupied, of course, by Napoleon Bonaparte and number one by Paul Sanderson who lives in Mid-Texas, 11 miles from anyone else, and doesn't take kindly to strangers.

This story concerns itself with Eilmer of Malmesbury, whose story involves his spotting of Halley's Comet in 1066. Eilmer addressed it with the words:

> "It is long since I saw you; but as I see you now you are much more terrible."

His greeting insinuated that he'd seen it before. To have done so, he would have had to have been born in the mid-980s, and so means that he would have attempted his most famous feat sometime in the early 1000s.

Ultimately Eilmer's life isn't well documented; we only know for certain that he is one of the earliest examples of a human being crafting a device (of sorts) and then attempting to fly.

Eilmer had read the Greek myth of Daedalus, who crafted wings for both him and his son Icarus to escape Crete. Interestingly, in the story, Daedalus warned Icarus not to fly too close to the sun, which he did and then plummeted to Earth. Eilmer believed the myth but seemed to have only listened to the first part that said, "create wings and fly", instead of the "that wasn't meant literally" in the second part.

Eilmer created wings and fastened them to himself in some fashion before climbing onto the roof of his abbey. He jumped off with the wings stretched out and reports say that he managed to catch a breeze

160

and do a bit of "flying," so to speak. He traveled around 218 yards before two things happened:

1. The wind changed direction violently, toppling him off course.
2. Eilmer became panicked because he was now flying, and he didn't know what to do.

Eilmer thus plummeted to Earth and broke both of his legs, losing his ability to walk. He went on to maintain that he would have succeeded had he included a tail. Perhaps - or perhaps the story of Daedalus isn't true, and one shouldn't attempt what one reads in Greek myths.

SWANNING AROUND LIKE THEY OWN THE PLACE

Britain is a country that has managed to hold onto a lot of outdated and strange laws that made sense when they were brought in but sound plain weird in the 21st century. For instance: being drunk in a pub is actually illegal and can get you a fine; you can't legally shake your rug in the street; and handling salmon in a suspicious manner can get you arrested. These laws were all reasonable additions to British society at the time they were written, but you'd be hard done by if a policeperson actually told you off for doing any of these things now.

Another famous "law," so to speak, is that the monarch of Britain *owns* all of its swans. The monarch can claim the swans if they choose to, although only a certain type of mute swan, not all swans as such. There's some evidence of the ruling that dates it to at least the 11th century CE. But some think it goes back even further. Like many things in history, there isn't a clear answer to the real question related to this ruling:

Why does the Monarch have this de facto dominion over these angry, feathered creatures?

However, the key seems to relate to status and power. Swans were seen as a delicacy, reserved only for the rich and, in particular, royalty. In 1247, Henry III ordered some 40 swans to be served for his Christmas dinner. Commoners were not allowed to even own swans, let alone eat them. Queen Elizabeth I, went through the Royal Court to decree that she owned all "royal fish" including swans, whales, porpoises, and sturgeons. That law still stands, by the way - in 2004, a man called Robert Davies caught a sturgeon and decided that it was only right to contact the royal household to make Queen Elizabeth II aware and to offer her the sturgeon. The Queen declined and told him he could use the fish "as he saw fit!"

Every year, in accordance with the importance of the swan, a five-day process known as "Swan Upping" is carried out. Groups of rowers capture swans on the River Thames and collect data on them such as their weight or injuries before fitting them with a tracking device if they don't yet have one.

It makes you wonder if it's true that they can even break a man's arm? Perhaps they just want you to stay away from the King's property...

WHO TURNED
OUT THE LIGHTS?!

It's not uncommon to be afraid of darkness. It's also not uncommon to be afraid of being stuck. So, therefore, it stands to reason that it's not uncommon to be afraid of the idea of being stuck underground. For French geologist Michel Siffre, that particular phobia didn't even dance across his mind when, in 1962, he spent two months in total isolation after shutting himself away in a subterranean cave.

Siffre was in his early twenties and a newly qualified scientist in the early 1960s when he happened on a genius idea (the jury's still out on that one) after planning an expedition into an underground glacier in the Alps. He was initially going to spend 15 days examining and "sciencing" in the glacier but just didn't feel like it would be enough time. In the end, he decided, in his own words:

"...to live like an animal, without a watch, in the dark, without knowing the time."

His sole research focus for the next decade was to observe how humans can function without light and without any definite concept of time. When he shut himself into the glacier, he had a few protocols to make sure that he didn't *die* while in there. He would call to a team by the entrance when he woke up, when he was going to sleep, and when he ate. The team couldn't call him at any point. The experiment showed, successfully, that humans have an internal body clock like other mammals.

Siffre spent his time reading and writing, but mainly he was thinking. Thinking of his future outside the cave and presumably, how much he'd love to get out. There were some interesting results in the isolated nightmare, mainly that his perception of time had become extremely warped during the two months. Every day he was asked to count 120 seconds, one digit per second, and it was found that his idea of how long 120 seconds was changed drastically. By September, he was experiencing five real minutes as though they were actually two. His experiment ended on September 14 and Siffre emerged, convinced that it had been called off early and that it was only mid-August!

Siffre puts the strange warping of time down to light and contends that if humans were entirely deprived of natural light, they'd lose most of their sense of how time actually passes by.

Siffre did many more isolation experiments throughout the 1960s, both with other scientists and on his own before performing his last experiment in 1972.

GHOST SHIPS ARE A THING OF THE PAST! RIGHT?

The phenomenon of a ghost ship is in itself a headscratcher. If you don't know, a ghost ship is a ship, boat, or vessel that is found floating in the water without any living crew on board. The most famous example remains as the fictional *Flying Dutchman*, a ghost ship that is doomed to sail the seven seas for all of the time, never to make port. There is no living crew operating the boat and the vessel is a sign of incoming peril for whatever unfortunate sailor spies it.

Though the *Flying Dutchman* doesn't really exist (apart from in *Pirates of the Caribbean*) the ghost ship phenomenon does and brings several strange stories with it. Some ghost ships are easily explained as being a ship that breaks free from the mooring and simply floats off. Someone finds it and is a bit spooked, but the explanation is that there's a furious old man living on the coast of Portugal who's lost his fishing boat. However, some seem more nefarious or just confusing. Here are but a few examples.

In October 1955, the *MV Joyita* departed Samoa with a full complement of crew members and passengers. The *Joyita* worked as a fishing and trading ship but was discovered in early November just north of Fiji, listing to the port side and missing its life rafts. The ship was in a very poor state, with corroded pipes, missing cargo, one working engine, and a faulty radio. The ship wouldn't sink, due to its extreme buoyancy, so why did no one remain on the vessel to await help? The enquiry found no good answer for what happened to the people on board, and their fate remains a mystery to this day.

Ever since 2011, dozens of empty ships have been arriving on Japanese shorelines from North Korea. Some of these boats hold the remains of crew members; many have nothing on board at all. Many of the ships are for fishing and are presumed to have been operating in oceans far away from their own country, due to overfishing near North Korea.

The working theory is that those on board weren't actually trained fishermen and soon become overwhelmed by the task of fishing in the Pacific Ocean. Either way, it's a strange and spooky phenomenon for those living on Japan's coastline. It also prompts the question: How many more boats are still bobbing around in the vast ocean?

The story of the ship called *Jenny* from the 19th century sounds as though it could be the plot of a 1950s horror movie (though admittedly, it lacks a bit of historical backing). The story goes that *Jenny* set sail from the Isle of Wight in 1823 and wasn't seen again for 17 years when it was discovered in the Drake Passage by the *Hope* and Captain Brighton in 1840. The ship was frozen in ice, along with its crew. Supposedly, the crew's bodies were in almost immaculate condition, preserved by the Antarctic chill. The logbook was taken by Captain Brighton for proof of what he had found.

There are dozens of stories about ghost ships, and they still occur in the 21st century. Have a surf for a few more on the internet, and hopefully avoid surfing into them in real life.

IT'S YOUR JOB TO WASH THE LOINCLOTHS, SON

You know those dreams in which you're inexplicably naked and everyone's pointing and laughing at you? Well, imagine that in real life, but everyone else is also naked, and presumably not laughing at you. Basically, imagine being naked. Got that? Good, let's continue.

If you happen to be in Inazawa, Japan on the 13th day of the lunar calendar, then you'll be lucky enough to watch thousands of men run around, fight, and sing in ceremonial loincloths and a splash of sake to battle the cold. The men will be seen parading around the normally quiet town, shouting rallying cries as buckets of icy water are launched all over the place in the event called Konomiya Hadaka Matsuri.

You'd probably be thinking, "Well, what's all this for?" The answer is that the men are waiting for the *shin-otoko*, "godman," a man who has been chosen to hold the honor before spending days in prayer and solitude to prepare. He's completely shaved when he emerges and is let loose into the festival wearing nothing but his dignity, which he may have also left behind.

From the moment that the *shin-otoko* arrives, the men will launch themselves at him, desperate to lay their hands on him in order to transfer their future misfortune and bad luck to him. As he nears the end of his…, run, he's pulled into the shrine and an almighty cheer rises to celebrate the success of the Konomiya Hadaka Matsuri, the Naked Man Festival. Later, the poor luck given to the *shin-otoko* is transferred into a black *mochi*, a type of cake, and buried in a secret location.

What is the point of all this? It's actually a religious occasion and is held in several different locations throughout Japan, not just Inazawa, usually in summer or winter. It's traditionally performed to guarantee luck, fortune, and a good harvest - but its potential blessings are numerous and varied. If you're down on your luck, maybe see if slapping your friend as they climb out of the bath does anything. You'll have a laugh at least.

OKAY, WHO ORDERED THE BANANA SUPREME WITH EXTRA BANANA AND BANANA FRIES?

A chimp's tea party. It's a rare saying that means that someone is making a massive mess while they eat food or drink, often said about children. Though in 20th-century Britain, a chimpanzee's tea party was a form of entertainment whereby the aforementioned primate was adorned in human clothing and provided with a "tea party" setting. They were, of course, banned in the 1970s because (a) it was cruel and (b) they were upsetting the custodians at London Zoo.

In Thailand, things are done a bit differently. Instead of creating a mocking display of chimps and laughing at them as they make a bit of a mess, in the ruins of the Phra Prang Sam Yot temple in Lopburi, a feast is laid out for macaque monkeys.

The whole thing is actually a festival, The Monkey Buffet Festival, with the monkey buffet being the main attraction. It's initiated by dancers in monkey costumes that welcome the audience as well as the guests of honor as the macaques arrive for their banquet. Once the guests have all sat at the correct name cards (not true), the sheets that covered the gargantuan amount of grub are removed and the macaques get stuck in.

The spread offers a colorful array of mainly fruit and vegetables such as watermelon, durian, lettuce, pineapple, and berries, coming to a grand weight of almost two tons.

The banquet is provided out of respect for monkeys that traces back two thousand years to the Hindu tale of Rama and Sita. In the story, the monkey king Hanuman helps Rama rescue his wife from a demon. Since then, among Hindus, monkeys have been associated with good luck and prosperity. So why not give them a slap-up meal?

If you visit, you are permitted to eat at nearby stalls and food vendors, not with the macaques. On the one hand, this is because it is unsanitary and against the conventions of the festival, and on the other, it's because the last thing you want is a jealous macaque bearing down on you after you took the last macadamia nut cookie.

"BLESS YOU! BLESS YOU! BLESS YOU! NOW PLEASE SHUT UP"

Sneezes are a lot like busses. They're difficult to predict, come two or more at a time, and there's normally a lot of attempted social distancing involved.

A sneeze is often cited as one of the more pleasurable bodily functions, right after defecating (at number one) and successfully canceling your phone contract without extra charges (a close second). What triggers sneezes in people is varied; external stimuli like pollen or light changes are common, while invisible bacteria or micro-amounts of dust can cause reactions too.

Interestingly, the first ever copyrighted footage in the United States of America was filmed on January 7, 1894, and is a simple series of 45 images of a man called Fred Ott sneezing. The occasion is celebrated as an important first step in cinematic history, despite its slightly odd content.

Most of us will sneeze approximately four times a day, ranging from small ahchoos to massive snot clearers. Unless of course the date is January 13, 1981, and your name is Donna Griffiths, a 12-year-old girl from Worcestershire, UK. On this seemingly normal day, Donna embarked on a *Guinness World Record*-certified journey that would take her 977 days to complete. The journey of *stopping* sneezing.

Donna began her sneezing fit in 1981 and then didn't stop sneezing until September 16, 1983, destroying the previous record of 194 days by a whopping 783 days. The reason for her impressive sneezing fit isn't confirmed as such, but there have been many cases before of people having extended *ahchoo* sessions, but none so impressive. All we can be sure of is that Donna was almost solely responsible for doubling Kleenex's profits in 1982 as well as leading to the banning of the phrase "Bless you" in Worcestershire.

DEAR ME, I AM PLEASED THAT I HAVE RESPONDED TO ME...

Allow this story to invade your brain-space, a space that occupies important things such as PINs and that website address, you're not supposed to visit. This story is about one of the most pointless exercises since an overly picky sailor began rearranging deckchairs on the sinking *Titanic*. We journey to the earliest days of modern American history, way back to 1789 as George Washington became the first President of the United States of America.

Washington is known for being a founding father, one of the first important people who helped to establish the United States as its own independent country. In effect, he's one of the most important people in history because of what the US went on to become, a world power, in effect an empire and dictator of global politics. He was also not very good at writing. Washington admitted it himself. He could, of course, write well, but he was no wordsmith - and when you're coming up with fundamental laws that will impact a country not only in the present but also in the future..., well, you should probably be able to write it.

This is why George Washington took on the services of the prominent politician, founding father, and advisor James Madison. Washington wanted his first contact with Congress to be perfect, inspiring, and clear. So, he asked James Madison to write it for him, which he did expertly and crafted history by doing so, initially inspiring confidence in the President.

You might be saying, "Why, nothing sounds pointless at all so far! This is a silly story, give me my money back!" Whoa there, pump the brakes.

In 1789, James Madison was not only a trusted advisor of George Washington but was also a member of Congress for Virginia. Congress, upon hearing the letter from Washington (written by

Madison), wanted to write a letter back to Washington to say how excited they were to work with him. The problem is, they needed a great writer to make sure that the letter was perfect, inspiring, and clear. So, James Madison was asked to write a letter on behalf of Congress in response to Washington. Which he did expertly.

So, the first correspondence between Washington and Congress was actually just James Madison writing to himself. But the story isn't yet done!

Washington decided to send a response to Congress, which Madison wrote and then Congress decided to respond to Washington's response to their response. Which Madison *also* wrote! All in all, Madison wrote four letters to himself, written by himself. Who knows how much Madison influenced the future of America by penning those first few letters...

HONOR EVEN IN WAR

War is no time for generosity and kindness, many would think. But in World War I there were several examples of a streak of humanity echoing across the vast stretches of barbarity and gross breaches of human rights. Famously, on Christmas Eve 1914, the German soldiers walked across no-mans-land to celebrate Christmas with the English and French soldiers. They played soccer, shared rations, and told stories before returning to shooting at each other within a day. It was also considered poor sportsmanship to shoot at pilots who were parachuting from planes; the pilot had already lost their air battle and it wasn't right to kill them if they'd survived. These are both relatively famous examples of how a bit of civility still existed in the theater of war.

A clearer example, however, can be found in the story of Captain Robert Campbell from Gravesend, UK who was captured as a Prisoner of War in July 1914. Prisoners of War are protected from certain abuses or should be anyway, and they receive some contact with the outside world even as war wages on.

By 1916, Campbell was 31 years of age and had received word that his mother Louise Campbell was sick and close to death. Campbell, overcome with grief that he wouldn't see his mother again, wrote a letter to Kaiser Wilhelm II begging the German Emperor to let him journey back to Gravesend to see his mother. Strangely, the Kaiser responded and said "Yes," or rather:

"Ja."

There was one condition: Campbell had to return within two weeks to the prison. He was asked to keep his word as an army officer. In December 1916, Campbell traveled to Gravesend and spent a week with his mother, while also presumably finding any old friends around to have several drinks with (if modern-day Gravesend is anything to go by). He then took a two-day trip via boat and train back to his prison, where he remained until the end of the war. His mother died in February 1917.

It's incredible to think that the Kaiser responded to the letter and even more incredible that he let Campbell go. After all, no one *made* him go back.

I HAVE THIS VOICE IN MY HEAD
THAT JUST WON'T LEAVE

Do you have voices in your head? Did you know that somewhere between 30–50% of people have an inner voice? Meaning that, in a minority, they have an actual voice in their head and hear many of their own thoughts as though they were being spoken. While the majority observe their own thoughts in a different way, they may be able to have an inner monologue, but it normally comes through actual effort.

If you're lucky enough to have an inner monologue, what does it tell you? Hopefully, if it's "kill, kill now!" Then you're seeking urgent assistance and please give our best to everyone in your new facility. Most likely, it is just mundane stuff, such as, "I might make a sandwich soon. I'm not sure if the Marvel Cinematic Universe can realistically carry on at the pace it has been. My neighbor is annoying." Normal things. But how would you react if that inner monologue started to say things like:

"You're in danger, go to hospital now."

This exact situation faced a woman whose name is undisclosed, but is referred to as AB and is from England.

In 1984, AB began hearing voices. Weirdly, they told her three pieces of information that turned out to be true. Rightfully freaked out, AB got help and underwent counseling and medication. Thankfully, her hallucinations receded. Unfortunately for AB, however, they returned shortly after while she was on vacation. It was now predominantly two voices that were giving her instructions.

The voices demanded that AB go back to England and abandon her holiday - they kept telling her something was wrong with her, and that she must return instantly. AB did so, unsure of the new phenomenon that was occurring inside of her. Once back in England, the voices told her that she must visit a certain address in London, which AB's husband agreed to drive her to after a small amount of persuasion. She was soon dropped off at the brain scan department of a prominent London hospital.

She demanded a brain scan, which the hospital granted. The scan showed that AB had a brain tumor, from which she fully recovered after an invasive operation.

As she regained consciousness, she heard the voices one final time as they said to her:

"We are pleased to have helped you. Goodbye."

The psychiatrist who initially treated her thinks that it's likely she felt a sensation in her head and her subconscious conjured the voices to get her to seek help. Either way, it's a spectacular bit of luck.

LA MANCHA NEGRA

Few things could convince me, definitively, that aliens are here on Earth. The man from Arkansas saying he saw "funny lights"? No. The reports from bored housewives in the '50s that they were abducted by a handsome spaceman? Uh-uh. A teenager who smoked marijuana while watching *Men In Black 2* and is now convinced that aliens work in post offices? Unfortunately, no.

But a black ooze that is slowly taking over Venezuelan roads, killing almost 2,000 motorists along the way, and leaving no definitive sign of what it is? Yeah, that'll do it.

The ooze is known as La Mancha Negra (The Black Stain) and first came to attention in 1986 in Caracas, Venezuela. It initially appeared as a black smudge, some 50 yards long, and was barely worthy of note. A group of construction workers commented on it, and it didn't take long for eight miles of highway to be covered in the strange material. By that time, a great deal of concern had begun to grow about what it was, as well as how to stop it.

The material has a gummy texture and renders the highway between Caracas and the airport unsafe at best. Cars career off of the road, or into each other, on contact with La Mancha Negra, and many lives have been claimed since the 1980s. By 1992, 1,800 deaths were attributed to the strange substance and it had spread across the city of Caracas.

The government announced that they would be pledging millions of dollars to investigate La Mancha *Negra* and to find a solution, bringing in expert advice from across the world. Through the 1990s, many methods were tried, such as: scraping the material, pressure washing it away, using chemicals, and destroying and repaving the roads. None of the methods worked; La Mancha Negra remained. German cleaning equipment was used in 1996 and seemed to do some damage to the material, but by 2001, the ooze was back in several areas across Venezuela.

No one knows yet what La Mancha Negra is. One thing's for sure, however: drive very slowly if you're in Venezuela. Also, don't follow the bright lights for fear of probing.

I THOUGHT WE WERE FRIENDS!

In the 1st century BCE, there was a problem with pirates. They seemed not to care a great deal about the reach of the Roman Empire and general law and order (imagine that!). The Mediterranean Sea in particular was a hotbed for piracy. Pirates were looting, pillaging, and downloading copies of *Game of Thrones* and showed no sign of stopping.

In 75 BCE, a group of pirates in the Aegean Sea took it all a step too far when they captured a young Roman nobleman by the name of Julius Caesar.

At this time, Caesar wasn't a well-known name outside of Rome, but he already held a fearsome reputation among many in the capital city. When Caesar was kidnapped, he essentially laughed in the pirates' faces as they informed him that his ransom would be 20 talents. He told them that if they knew who they'd captured then they'd make it 50.

Caesar settled in as a prisoner with a quiet sense of humble dignity. Oh, wait, no he didn't. Caesar adopted the role of demi-captain, parading around the ship giving orders to sailors, and criticizing how the ship was being run from top to bottom. Caesar wrote while he was in "captivity" and demanded that the pirates listen to his poetry and writing. If they didn't like it then he'd call them stupid or illiterate for failing to grasp his genius. Caesar did participate in games with the pirates but would consistently act as though he was the captain, something the pirates found oddly endearing about their prisoner.

Throughout his stay, Caesar routinely threatened the pirates with a painful death in the near future. They laughed it off as the posturing of an uninfluential Roman noble, but they couldn't have been more wrong.

After 38 days, Caesar was released from his strange punishment, and he quickly raised a naval force to hunt down the pirates. He found them and brought them to the authorities in Asia, but the governor was hesitant to enact too much vengeance on behalf of Caesar, so bad was the pirate problem. Caesar essentially said, "Fine, I'll do it myself," and had them all crucified.

The only way any of the pirates could have gotten the last laugh here would have been to whisper to another, as they were hanging there, "Who's this dude again?"

EVERYONE HAS A LITTLE BIT
OF BART SIMPSON DEEP DOWN

Do you trust 15-year-olds? Well, if you do then you shouldn't. If you don't know why then ask any parent with a child who's now in their twenties and they'll provide you with five reasons.

Allow us to examine one such case that might provide further insight: the early life of Aisin-Gioro Puyi, the last Emperor of China. He inherited the throne at just two years old in 1908. Puyi, as he is best known, was a spoilt young child. Yes, he was surrounded by advisors trying to tell him how best to rule, given his youth, but ultimately, he was doted on by absolutely everyone. It's helpful to have the ruler of China like you; it's even more helpful if all you have to do is pass him some candy now and again.

Due to the almost total lack of discipline, Puyi became unruly and developed little sense of what was right, moral, or kind. This came out in behaviors that one might deem to be childish hijinks. You know, flogging servants, shooting people with an air gun, and attempting to bake a cake filled with iron filings because you "want to see what it looks like when they eat it." Yeah, hijinks.

All these rather perverse behaviors aside, which Puyi himself later admitted were troubling, at the age of 15, Puyi proved why boundaries are so important for children and teens.

The telephone was a recent invention and highly exciting. *Puyi* learned of the technology through a tutor of his and demanded that one be installed in his quarters. His advisors were afraid of what might happen should he have access to the outside world, so tried to tell him that it was unnecessary to have one at this stage of his life, but he was insistent. He wanted to talk to people who weren't just yes-men or avid worshippers. Perhaps other leaders could provide further insight as to how best to command his vast empire. Or at least, that's how he might have justified it.

In reality, Puyi, the ruler of one of the most important nations in human history, used his phone to make prank calls, which he found hilarious. He famously used to phone random restaurants and phone in massive orders to be delivered to random addresses. He also phoned celebrities such as musicians and singers, giggled when they answered, then hung up doubled-over in laughter.

He was only one step away from asking if anyone knows a "Hugh Jass" at the nearest temple!

PINEAPPLE INSURANCE MIGHT BE SENSIBLE AT THAT PRICE

In the 1700s and 1800s, pineapples were seen as exotic luxuries and carried a hefty price tag. In the colonies of America in the early 1700s, a pineapple would run a cost of approximately $8,000 (in modern-day value).

They were seen as such a luxury because pineapples can only really be grown in tropical environments, hence why they are native to South America and were later imported to be grown in the Caribbean. To access pineapples in the 1700s and 1800s, Europeans would have them imported across vast distances onboard a ship. By the time they arrived, though, many would be moldy and bruised. It took until the mid-17th century for pineapple-growing conditions to be correctly mimicked in hothouses in Europe, thus making them able to be grown closer to the consumers' homes. But they were still rare and a talking point for nobility.

At dinner parties, it became common to have a pineapple as the centerpiece of the table so the hosts could show just how darn wealthy they were. Any guests would be impressed. It was a bit like someone today displaying their polished Tesla prominently on the drive as dinner guests walk into the party - it's to show that they can afford the expensive thing. It impresses the sort of person who wishes beyond all else that *they* could afford the expensive thing.

At the start of the 20th century, pineapples began to be mass-produced by a company operating out of Hawaii, which drastically damaged the popularity and perceived "classiness" of the exotic fruit among the upper classes. Nowadays, displaying a pineapple just tells your guests:

"I'm planning on eating a pineapple later."

185

THE RHYTHM IS GONNA GETCHA! GETCHA INTO THE GRAVE!

You know those nights at the club, where you feel like you could happily boogie forever, and the music is absolutely superb and the beverages plentiful? Your friend might even turn to you at some stage and say:

> *"This is great, I never want to stop dancing…, now where's the toilet, I'm going to vomit."*

Well, in 1518 a bizarre epidemic of dancing took hold of the citizens of Strasbourg such that they couldn't bring themselves to stop their dancing…, literally.

The Dancing Plague of 1518 remains a bit of a mystery as to its causes and effects but is quite funny. For some reason, in July 1518, people started dancing (it was kicked off by a woman whose name is disputed) and for approximately five to six weeks, up to 400 people danced away relentlessly. The Strasbourgians were unable to explain why they were dancing, but the government ultimately had to intervene and committed the dancers to the hospital so that they could cease their incessant cha-cha'ing under medical supervision.

The explanations at the time were largely accusations of witchcraft or demonic possession, driven by the mass hysteria around superstition that existed in early 16th-century Europe. More modern assessments speculate about food poisoning from rotten food consumption or a mass hysteria caused by a recently stressful few years for the citizens of Strasbourg. Regrettably, no explanation is taken as the definitive answer yet, and it's likely we may not ever truly know. Although, it's bizarre that no one has suggested that a local bard could simply have been playing an outrageously good song that you couldn't *not* dance to!

Some historians have asserted that the dancing led to death from exhaustion, with sources suggesting that 10–15 people were dying every day. However, the figures weren't recorded at the time, so either there were no deaths, or the officials were jigging too much to write.

WATCHING CLOWNS ONLY LANDS YOU IN TROUBLE, OR THE RIVER

The year is 1845 and society is yet to realize that clowns are scary, creepy, unsettling, and evil. It wasn't really their fault; in 1845, most entertainment was all of the above with an added element of danger thrown in. That's proven by the disaster at the Yarmouth Suspension Bridge on May 2, 1845.

Cooke's Royal Circus was in Great Yarmouth, on the east coast of Great Britain, and that was huge news. Cooke's Royal Circus was a major attraction in the 19th century, promising strongmen, acrobats, equestrian acts, and of course, clowns. As part of the promotion effort to bring customers in to watch the incredible circus, it was announced that Arthur Nelson, a wonderful clown, would be sailing up the River Bure in a washtub with four geese pulling him along. A crowd gathered at 5 p.m. to watch, ready to be amused and especially ready to part with their hard-earned money.

Most watched from the riverbank, while a crowd of 300 looked on from the Yarmouth Suspension Bridge. The bridge wasn't full by any means - carts were able to pass by - but it was still a larger than-usual number of people to have on the bridge. At 5:40 p.m. one of the crucial eyebars on the bridge failed. Several crowd members witnessed this occur and immediately…, *didn't* raise the alarm! No one evacuated the bridge, they instead decided to continue to watch the bizarre clown performance in front of them.

A second eyebar collapsed within five minutes, and the bridge's structure began to crumble. The south side of the bridge fell into the river along with the crowd that had been standing there, transfixed by the clown. Hundreds tumbled into the seven-foot-deep water, along with a great deal of rubble.

Unfortunately, 79 people died in the tragedy, with 59 of that number being children. If anyone asks you to go and watch a clown do *anything,* say no - they cause calamity all around them. If it's not a pie in the face, it's a bridge collapsing.

IT'S A CONDITION CALLED
IMANALCOHOLICITIS

Prohibition America sounds like it was simultaneously overwhelmingly boring and unbelievably exciting at the same time. Prohibition was a period during the 1920s when alcohol was banned in the United States. Citizens were not allowed to buy any more than they already owned and that was that! Everyone went sober for years...

Just kidding! In response to the ban, speakeasies opened in major cities across America. These were secret bars where alcohol was sold, often run by gangsters. Police themselves even drank there while off duty and many adults knew how to get themselves into at least one secret bar. Other people just got better at hiding it. It was during this period that the Long Island Iced Tea was invented. The LIIT is a cocktail of several spirits and lemon juice, mixed with Coca-Cola. It looks a bit like a simple, harmless iced tea - but is absolutely lethal if in the hands of an aunt at a wedding. The trades of alcohol smuggling and home-brewing became heavily practiced, with consumption of the illegal alcohol moonshine soaring.

So, all in all, not everyone was sticking to the rules, least of all politicians from other countries.

Winston Churchill visited America in 1932, while the prohibition was still in effect. With regard to the Prime Minister's drinking habits, "Churchill had always enjoyed a drink" is a polite way of putting it; "Churchill was a functioning alcoholic" is the correct way. Luckily, he managed to secure a quite brilliant letter from his doctor to help bypass the legislation. That was handy, since as such a public figure, he wouldn't be able to ignore the rules as brazenly as the ordinary Joe. His doctor's note read thusly:

> *"This is to certify that the post-accident convalescence of the Hon. Winston S Churchill necessitates the use of alcoholic spirits especially*

at meal times. The Quantity is naturally indefinite but the minimum requirements would be 250 cubic centimeters."

So, Churchill could legally indulge in endless amounts of booze while the American citizens had to pretend that they weren't. What a mad, lawless jungle it was. It's worth pointing out that Churchill visited speakeasies on his visit all the same! Supposedly, he was "investigating."

OLIVER "SCROOGE MCGRINCH" CROMWELL

Oliver Cromwell remains a controversial figure in Britain to this day for many reasons including his barbarity, mistreatment of Irish people, and spearheading of a violent revolution. But we won't focus on that right now because this is a silly, funny book. Cromwell is often seen as a "grumpy old man" because he supposedly banned Christmas after becoming Lord Protector in 1653, four years after beheading Charles I.

The story of Cromwell banning Christmas is full of red herrings and misunderstandings, but at the very least, he was partially to blame for the ending of the most jovial time of the year for many.

By the 1640s, the Puritan way of life, which advocated more "back to basics" Christianity, was experiencing a wave of popularity in England. It was all about ensuring that holy days remained holy, restricting baser pleasures, and keeping God closer to people's hearts. In 1643, under Charles I, an ordinance was passed encouraging all subjects to consider what Christmas is about - that is, as a holy day and not one for drinking lots or vomiting on the streets of London on the back of your horse. This did not work, and in 1644 a separate ordinance was passed that banned the feast of Christmas and other celebrations entirely.

As Cromwell became a more influential figure (and eventually ruler), he instigated rules that made the whole "no-Christmas" thing more concrete. Soldiers patrolled London, shutting down any sign of people selling food that was prepared for any Christmas celebration. Until 1660, Christmas was a day for quiet contemplation and prayer, not for levity, feasting, and drinking. In other words, Christmas was boring for about 15 years and though it wasn't all his fault, Cromwell was certainly partially to blame.

THE SPAGHETTREE

You may find this hard to believe, but in Britain in the 1950s, the British people weren't particularly knowledgeable about the world of good food. This must come as a shock, after all, Britain is the country that has brought the world such culinary delights as jellied eels, Spam, and the deep-fried Mars Bar! But in the '50s, not much was known about global cuisine and the BBC used this lack of knowledge to stage a prank on April Fools' Day that CNN called:

> "...the biggest hoax that any reputable news establishment ever pulled."

The 1957 news report presented a family in Switzerland who were excited about a bumper harvest of spaghetti due to the disappearance of the "spaghetti weevil." The rest of the broadcast focused on a festival celebrating the huge harvest as well as describing the selective breeding processes behind achieving the perfect strand of spaghetti. Employing respected broadcaster Richard Dimbleby to narrate the story was masterful; his voice added an air of authenticity to the narrative and many people bought the crazy, contrived spiel and took it as absolute fact.

At the time, pasta wasn't a common food item in Britain like it is today, and most people viewed it as exotic. They wouldn't have known how it was produced, so the story was believable in the eyes of many. The BBC reported that many people phoned up asking where they could get their own Spaghetti Tree so that they could have their own harvest. After all, no spaghetti weevils had been found in England yet!

The BBC responded, "Place a sprig of spaghetti in a tin of tomato sauce and hope for the best."

I'm still waiting for mine to flower.

A PLACE TO PAYYOUR RES-POO-CTS

If you mention the name George S. Patton to an American history buff, then they may give a far-off look of reverence and respect in response. George Patton was a general in the US Army during World War II in his fifties and fought in World War I in his twenties. As well as being a military legend, Patton shows us just how embarrassing a situation can be if you don't simply speak up when you should.

In 1917, Patton was stationed in the French town of Bourg where he had established the headquarters of his Tank Brigade. By this stage, he was at the rank of captain, seen as a fantastic leader on the Western Front, and oversaw the training of many soldiers in the newly-established method of tank warfare. To Patton's shock, one day the mayor approached him in tears. Patton consoled the mayor who asked why Patton had failed to mention that one of his soldiers had recently died.

Patton paused and responded that none of his soldiers had died, to his knowledge. The mayor mentioned that the soldier was in his grave, so Patton followed him to the burial site, presumably slightly anxious that he'd missed out on something so important as the death of someone in his command. When they reached the grave, Patton saw an old latrine pit (basically a hole that soldiers "do their business" in) with a makeshift, joke cross-sign on it with the inscription "Abandoned Rear."

Patton was too embarrassed to correct the mayor for mourning a toilet, so remained quiet to preserve the man's dignity.

Patton revisited the town in 1944 during the next World War for a hit of morbid nostalgia and was shocked to discover that the grave site for Abandoned Rear still remained and was being maintained by the locals, who had come to see the unknown soldier as a hero. Patton once again didn't correct anyone and took the secret to the grave with him. The true story only came out when his memoirs were published after his death.

"I APOLOGIZE PROFUSELY FOR DOING EXACTLY AS ASKED"

(<u>Warning</u>: content that will be confusing if you haven't had decent sexual education)

The human reproductive system isn't much of a mystery and hasn't ever really been. Humans know that it takes a man and a woman to have reproductive intercourse. The man releases sperm (given anywhere from 30 seconds to two minutes) and, all going well, a baby comes along nine months later. For a large part of human history, that was about all anyone could work out due to a lack of technology that explained what was happening at a microscopic level. The first person to discover what was actually happening beneath the surface was microbiologist Antoine Philips van Leeuwenhoek who, in the 17th century, took a microscope to a sperm sample.

Leeuwenhoek had been urged to examine sperm several times during his life, due to his marvelous innovations in microscopic technology. He refused time and time again, he said because of his religious beliefs. In reality, it's probably because he was a bit grossed out and just didn't want to have to involve himself with the process. He gave in to the pressure from the *Royal Society*, a group of academics that received patronage from the English monarchy to publish important scientific findings of the time. Leeuwenhoek sat at his desk with his sample and gazed through his wonderful microscope (presumably with a wince). What he found was bizarre.

It transpired that sperm was made up of a load of a quite strange-looking worm sort of things that were actually *alive*!? They were moving, at any rate! Leeuwenhoek was aghast at the discovery and felt quite unwell. He had never been much of a scientific thinker, he was more of an observer, so he couldn't put his religious-based disgust out of his head as he gazed at the strange microorganisms. This attitude is shown in his hilariously prudish correspondence with the Royal Society.

Initially, Leeuwenhoek apologized and informed the society that they can essentially pretend it never happened:

> *"If your Lordship should consider that these observations may disgust or scandalise the learned, I earnestly beg your Lordship to regard them as private and to publish or destroy them as your Lordship sees fit."*

Imagine one of the most innovative scientists of his day saying, "I'm so sorry, but this is revolting, shall we pretend that I didn't see anything?" Even better than this panicky writing, however, was that Leeuwenhoek felt the need to assert that he hadn't obtained the sample through "sinful contrivance," but it was simply "the excess which Nature provided me." I'm sure the Royal Society of learned men were thinking, "Yeah, thanks for that, buddy, I really didn't need to know."

It took many years for an actual investigation to take place on what the job of sperm was. The Royal Society weren't all that interested, truth be told. Perhaps they just told Leeuwenhoek to do it as a joke, knowing it would upset him. Rumor goes that they then asked Isaac Newton to put his bum in a printing press to see how it turned out.

STOP, THINK, AND STOP AGAIN, THEN LOOK, THEN STOP

Perhaps you've heard of the Darwin Awards? A Darwin Award is a joke honor given out to people who have died in particularly stupid ways and therefore have contributed to human evolution by no longer being a part of it. A bit cruel at times, perhaps, but there is a certain humor to be found in the way that some people shuffle off this mortal coil. Here are a select few slightly morbid true stories, nominees, and winners of the never coveted award:

- In 1997, Eric Barcia was found dead after attempting to bungee jump from a 70-foot bridge. Eric had taken all safety precautions into his own hands and so tied several cords together that came to a length of just under 70 feet. Of course, forgetting that bungee cords stretch…
- In 2022, a young man crashed into a parked car in San Diego and died almost instantly. He was stirring a protein shake with a sharp knife, veered to the right, hit the car with no one in it, and stabbed himself. At some point, you must just stop and think, "Hang on, is this a bad idea?"
- In 2017, in Japan, a warehouse worker was faced with a logistical problem. How to change a lightbulb that was 32 feet off of the ground, especially if your forklift only reaches 8 feet? Well, the answer is to stack approximately 40 wooden pallets on top of each other, place yourself on top, and get your friend to raise the pallets to the ceiling, enabling you to change the bulb. The stack collapsed and he died almost instantly.
- In 1992, an employee at the Pancake Pantry in Nashville decided that he would rob the establishment while it was closed. He climbed on top of the roof and gazed down the exhaust chute that hung over the grill. It seemed too tight, so he decided to take all of his clothes off and slide down. As he did

so, he got his arm caught under his own chin, suffocating himself and dying with *that* being the last thing he ever did.

There's far more to mention and the morbid humor is quite something to behold, as is the tireless work of those who give the awards. For more, it's worth a visit to www.darwinawards.com

INTRODUCING ADMIRAL DR PEPPER AND CAPTAIN FANTA

Did you know that in 1989 Pepsi possessed a strong naval force that could have started an invasion against almost any country and would have certainly beaten Belgium? The story is peculiar but, despite its intrigue, it's still unacceptable to ever answer "Yes" to the question "We don't have Coke, is Pepsi, okay?"

The Cold War had rumbled on from the end of World War II until 1991, marked by constant competition between the Soviet Union and America. It was *extremely* tense and international relations couldn't have been much worse. There seemed to be no end in sight, and given how World War II had ended in Japan, both sides were wary of the potential repercussions if anyone did a bit more than just threatened.

Enter Don Kendall, the CEO of Pepsi aged 42 in 1963. Don was an entrepreneurial fella, and he'd observed Coca-Cola's global success. They were quickly leaving PepsiCo behind. With markets in Europe, Asia, and America all dominated by Coca-Cola, it was no competition. But in the end, Kendall won, and now Pepsi is bigger - said no one, ever. However, in 1963, there was one place that Coca-Cola did not dominate, the Soviet Union. In fact, it wasn't sold there at all.

Kendall managed to get a spot at the American National Exhibition in 1959 where there was to be an attempted reconciliation in the relationship between the two countries. He saw the perfect opportunity to put PepsiCo on the map. Nikita Khrushchev and Richard Nixon were wandering around, observing the different products on display and they stopped at Kendall's stand. Kendall offered Khrushchev a sip and the Russian leader adored it. The PepsiCo boss was probably punching the air at this point, but unfortunately for him, the exhibition wasn't quite the roaring success that it could have been.

Throughout the 1960s, relations between the two countries deteriorated to the worst they'd ever been and even Kendall, desperate for his own glory, didn't desire to upset the American government - so he sat on his initial Soviet success. He finally made his move in 1971, when he officially confirmed trade with the Soviet Union and the communist union began importing Pepsi. It sold exceptionally well. The people absolutely loved it (it does mix well with Vodka), and the exporting units made Kendall a very successful man.

However, being an American company, PepsiCo were not legally allowed to accept money from the USSR, so the USSR traded them the vodka brand Stolichnaya instead, allowing PepsiCo to sell it and pocket the cash. Stolichnaya quickly became America's favorite vodka and the money rolled in on this convoluted trade deal. Frustratingly, by the late 1980s, the deal was faltering. Stolichnaya wasn't selling in America as well as Pepsi was in Russia and PepsiCo was considering ending the deal. Sensing that disaster was on the way, in 1989, the Soviet government came up with an ingenious solution to grant PepsiCo the following:

A cruiser, a frigate, a destroyer, 17 submarines, and several oil tankers

That meant that, in 1989, Pepsi boasted the world's sixth-largest naval force. The US government were furious at this bizarre deal, but Kendall responded to their strong criticism with great wit:

"I'm dismantling the Soviet Union faster than you are."

And so, everyone clapped. Not really, but in their minds they did.

WHAT DO THEY PLAN ON DOING WITH IT?

If you pull out your nearest atlas, globe, or app depicting our planet and look slightly north of Greenland, and slightly south of Ellesmere Island, Canada, then you'll see a passage of water known as the Nares Strait. Inside *that* strait, you'll observe a *tiny* island that has an area of approximately half a mile. This small piece of land is called Hans Island and is the site of a land dispute between Denmark and Canada that has taken over 50 years to settle.

Hans Island has very little value in and of itself. The land isn't some fount of natural resources, nor home to anything of spiritual importance; it has traditionally been used as Inuit hunting grounds. The dispute isn't really about whereby either Canada or Denmark can claim the land due to its importance. It's more of a staring contest where the stakes are so drastically low that very few people could even point to where the dispute might be on a map.

Denmark currently deals with all the foreign affairs of Greenland and has done since the 1930s. At this time, Denmark decreed that due to Hans Island's proximity to Greenland, they too own the small rock. And no one really seemed to mind. You may as well have asked - "do you prefer water at 53 degrees Fahrenheit or 57 degrees?" Only the very particular would have minded, and even then, they'd only be holding an opinion to be difficult.

It wasn't until the 1970s that any sort of dispute opened up. This happened when the coordinates for Hans Island were agreed upon by Canadian and Danish personnel. Upon publication of the coordinates, both Canada and Denmark claimed that the island rested in their jurisdiction and after much toing and froing, neither government could agree on who was right. An agreement was formed, with help from the UN, concerning borders in the strait, but no borders were drawn in Hans Island.

The two governments worked together, almost passive-aggressively, to allow research to take place throughout the 1980s and 1990s, with both Danish and Canadian flags being planted and removed in favor of the other's flag. Media attention was brought to the island in the 2000s as outlets found the undecided argument rather funny (but why? It's so normal and not weird!) and greater pressure emerged for something to happen.

Several advertisements began to turn up on *Google*, sponsored by Danish and Canadian pranksters (or perhaps governments), that claimed sovereignty for either nation. It wasn't until 2018 that the two countries formed a joint task force to decide what to do, once and for all.

In 2022, the two countries signed an agreement that split the island almost entirely in half along a natural fault. So that is that.

Just wait until someone tells the Canadians that they own less of the island than Greenland does...

WE HAD YOUR CAKE
AND ATE IT. SORRY.

Is there a more stereotypically cartoonish prank than some ruffians stealing food from a housewife after they left it to cool on the windowsill, rushing off into the sunset with a steaming pie, licking their lips, and chuckling away at the perfectly executed crime? Well, for Meri Mion this wasn't a scenario reserved for cartoons; it was simply something that happened in her real life in the final days of World War II.

Mion was a young girl in 1945, only 13 years old when in the final days of the war her town of San Pietro witnessed an outbreak of violence between American and German soldiers. Mion escaped to the attic with her mother to hide from the volleys of bullets in her hometown and waited for the fighting to cease.

Her mother decided that she'd make Mion a birthday cake, hoping that that would help settle some jittery nerves. She baked it up and left it to cool by the windowsill (had she not read a comic ever?!) and they both went about their days, waiting to celebrate the occasion properly in the evening.

Unfortunately, some passing American soldiers saw the opportunity, nabbed the cake from the windowsill, and made off with it. Like a gang of Dennis the Menaces, off they went into the sunset with their prize. This left Mion disappointed on the day, but with a funny story to tell, nonetheless.

Satisfyingly, the story has a happy ending. In April 2022, the US Army formally gave a birthday cake to Mion at a ceremony in Vicenza to commemorate the fighting, the dead, and the cakes forgotten along the way. The US Army said the whole ordeal is a little embarrassing but at least they were able to put it right as Mion turned 90.

Though it would have been funnier if the Colonel offered it to her, then snatched it back shouting, "nyer, nyer!" before running off into the hills to eat it all like a greedy little boy.

WE DIDN'T MEAN UNLIMITED!
WE MEANT "UNLIMITED"!

American Airlines made a mistake in 1981, one that someone high up should have seen would eventually lead to problems. They offered a **"LIFETIME UNLIMITED AAIRPASS"** – that's right, an unlimited ticket! The tickets were calculated based on your age, with the most famous case being Steven Rothstein purchasing one for $250,000. You could also purchase a "companion" ticket, for someone to come with you. Rothstein purchased this at $150,000. For $400,000, Steven Rothstein had bought unlimited flights for the rest of his life for himself plus one, and boy did he use them.

Rothstein was a family man who already was one of American Airlines' most frequent fliers when he purchased the unlimited ticket in 1981, but now he was taking journeys every time he was able. He'd take a child on holiday while he attended business meetings or take a family member out of state for a weekend. In general, he lived with American Airlines. He grew to know every staff member he met: the security, the departure lounge workers, the greeters, and the cabin crew. He journeyed excessively throughout the rest of the 20th century and into the 21st, ensuring that he was taking full advantage of the innumerable miles he had at his disposal.

The problem was that come the 21st century, someone at *American Airlines* noticed that the passengers who owned these Lifetime Unlimited AAirpasses were costing the airline an outrageous amount of money for no benefit. They were literally making no money on these customers, but some were costing them over a million dollars per year. Superb job, well done, great business.

So, they began to investigate these passengers for "fraudulent use" of their passes. The company were clearly desperate to end the privileges if they could and successfully managed to in many cases. Rothstein was simply told one day when he went to get on a flight that his pass no longer worked because of his activity with the account.

Gob smacked, Rothstein learned that the company had considered writing him a letter to warn him in advance but didn't want the poor press. Rothstein went on to publicly drag the company over the coals for not abiding by the terms of their pass. He attempted to sue them for $7 million. American Airlines fought back and attempted to sue Rothstein in return for allegedly misusing the pass. The case was *very* public, making it onto the front page of many international newspapers and lasting years, creating a perception of American Airlines as a money-grabbing corporation that didn't care about its customers. Where did anyone get that from?

In the end, Steven Rothstein lost. He *had* made some odd purchases using his pass that were difficult to prove *weren't* misuses of his privileges, and he was awarded no monetary value. But the ticket had likely already paid for itself several times over by the time it was rescinded. So, if you see *anywhere* offer "unlimited" whatever, take it.

Of course, in the 21st century, deals like this wouldn't be offered anymore. It'd be a $15,000 per month subscription service with additional optional benefits such as a seat for only $999 extra per month. Doesn't sound bad, does it?

ARIANA GRANDE'S BBQ FINGER AND GRILL

If you're not one to pay much attention to showbiz stories or celebrity gossip then there's a chance that this story may have passed you by. For those a bit more clued in, you're likely very well aware of where this goes, but it is very funny, so it's worth reading again regardless.

In 2019, Grande released her single "7 Rings," and it achieved global success (like everything that Ariana Grande does, to be fair). She wanted to commemorate the song by getting a tattoo. She wanted the words "7 Rings" in Japanese on the palm of her hand and the result was thus:

七輪

But...this doesn't mean "7 Rings." What it actually means is "shichirin," a small Japanese barbecue grill.

Grande's followers quickly informed her that her tattoo was incorrect and the popstar sought to make things right. She messaged her Japanese tutor about what went wrong, and she was informed that with a few minor amendments the tattoo would read "seven finger circle," which is "7 rings" in Japanese. Happy days!

Grande went to get the tattoo changed, incurring a great deal of agony for herself as palm tattoos are notoriously painful for even the most seasoned of tattoo-getters. She proudly posted the new tattoo and thanked everyone involved for helping her reach the end of the debacle and cracked several jokes at her own expense. Many people thought "Oh, well done, that's sorted that out," but those people who thought that clearly couldn't read Japanese. Unfortunately, her new tattoo didn't read "7 Rings" either.

As Japanese is read vertically as well as left to right, the placement of the new characters on Grande's palm actually denoted the phrase

"Japanese barbecue finger." Ariana Grande continues to laugh about the story and now you can laugh along with her.

MAYBE SHARKNADO ISN'T THAT UNREALISTIC

Flightless animals falling from the sky sounds like a sign of an incoming apocalypse, or perhaps a bad reaction to some quite strong medication, but it's actually a recorded phenomenon that has happened several times across human history. The problem is that no scientific recording of animals falling from the sky exists, meaning we aren't totally sure why it happens, though there are some likely theories.

When we discuss a Rain of Animals, we don't just mean an unlucky mouse who has been dropped by a falcon somewhere over British Columbia. That one little guy isn't a Rain, it's a droplet. What we mean by a "Rain" is many animals, often the same ones, falling in a given location as if living, breathing precipitation.

In Singapore, in 1861, a Rain of Fish was reported. During a three-day-long bout of torrential rain, catfish were found in puddles around Singapore. It was suggested by a particularly overzealous naturalist called Francis Castelnau that a species of catfish had developed the ability to walk and were simply walking out of the ocean. A theory that, for some reason, has failed to gain traction as viable. Probably because it's a stupid thing to say.

The Roman naturalist Pliny the Elder documented storms of fish and frogs in the 1st century CE. They supposedly rained from the sky, along with massive amounts of rain. A drawing from 1660 by artist Erasmus Francisci suggests that there was a rain of snakes, though this doesn't really prove nor even suggest that anything of the sort really happened.

In these instances of fish and frogs (and snakes?), it's generally thought that a particularly strong wind or storm picked up the animals and deposited them elsewhere. Or a gust pushed them along, to where they oughtn't be, giving the impression that they are literally raining from the sky. While this is still undisputed, it formed the basic concept for the hit B-movie *Sharknado*, a documentary about what would happen if sharks were picked up instead of catfish (it's definitely not a documentary).

So, if you see a fish bobbing about somewhere it shouldn't be, then don't panic - it's either a recent storm, God's might, or your mad neighbor dropping fish about on their way back from the shops.

GET THAT MONKEY SOME TROUSERS! AND WHERE'S THE LLAMA'S DIAPER?

It's fair to say that people can be easily dragged into what is called a "moral panic." This is a widespread feeling of fear, shared by many people, which is often irrational and based on the idea that one thing threatens the community at large. Famous examples include the Satanic Panic in 1980s America, where parents became convinced that teenagers were becoming possessed by anti-Christian, demonic influences due to the emergence of the board game *Dungeons & Dragons*, as well as hard-rock music. The mass hysteria led parents to shut their children inside, enforce curfews and, in extreme cases, demand jail time for innocent teenagers who were simply playing a game.

Moral panics can be quite funny. They often involve a group of people being led along an unhelpful path that could be easily explained away if anyone stopped to think for even one second. One such brilliant example comes from 1959 with the creation of the Society for Indecency to Naked Animals (SINA).

SINA was actually an elaborate hoax created by Alan Abel, a filmmaker, and Buck Henry, a comedian. They presented a series of press releases detailing the history of SINA as a serious organization that was concerned with preserving the modesty of animals, to maintain a sense of Christian morality in American society.

They dreamt up slogans such as:

"A nude horse is a rude horse!"

They campaigned for the message that animals that stand at a height of more than four inches or longer than six inches require clothing so as not to offend the eyes of those moral Americans. One should be able to look at this and shake their head, thinking that it's either a joke or someone who has lost all sight of what being a Christian is. One doubts that God commanded Noah to make sure he had blouses prepared for the giraffes before they boarded the Ark.

Yet SINA grew in popularity rapidly, and many people attempted to donate money to the cause. Both Abel and Henry returned the money in all cases so as not to be charged with fraud at a later date. Publicly they said that they wanted the "charity" to remain free and to simply complete the good work it was attempting to carry out. Tens of thousands of supporters joined the cause before the hoax was exposed in 1962 as people had begun to recognize Buck Henry as a comedian and many people were furious about the everlasting prank. Many more, however, chuckled at the silly charity but more so at the tens of thousands who'd managed to get themselves wound up over something that is not a problem and never will be.

13 YULE LADS

If you ask a child "What would be better than Father Christmas?" The only truthful response would be to confidently announce "10 FATHER CHRISTMASES!" If you're a child in Iceland, this is not just a fantasy, but a very real possibility. The children of Iceland are lucky enough to enjoy 13 Father Christmases!

In Iceland, the bringers of cheers are called the Yule Lads and they visit, one by one, in the 13 nights leading up to Christmas. The children leave out a shoe for each Lad and the Lad either leaves candy if the child has been good or rotting potatoes if they've behaved poorly throughout the year.

The Lads are quite mischievous and aren't just jolly large fellows with booming voices. During the Medieval period, parents used the Lads to scare their children into behaving well, alongside stories of the Christmas Cat who prowled around on Christmas Eve, eating anyone who was not wearing one piece of new clothing. The Lads used to be depicted in quite horrifying ways, though from the 1800s onward, they became cheekier, playing harmless tricks on naughty people.

The 13 Lads, of course, have different personalities, much like the Seven Dwarfs. Here's a basic description of the Lads. Perhaps you can use them in place of Coca-Cola's Santa Claus when you want children (yours or otherwise) to do as they are told. They are all a bit peculiar but bear in mind that they were devised hundreds of years ago. These descriptions are taken from the National Museum of Iceland:

1. Sheep-Cote Clod, who suckles farmers' yews in sheds.
2. Gully Hawk, who steals the foam from buckets of cow's milk (have better aspirations Gully Hawk, come on).
3. Spoon Licker, who...you can probably work it out.
4. Pot Licker, who takes unclean pots and cleans them with his tongue.

5. Door Slammer, who slams doors, preventing people from sleeping.
6. Skyr Gobbler, who eats all the Icelandic yogurt known as *skyr*.
7. Stubby, who is short and steals food.
8. Sausage Swiper, who steals sausages.
9. Window Peeper, who enjoys peering through people's windows and sometimes steals what he sees.
10. Meat Hook, who steals any meat that's been left out.
11. Bowl Licker, who steals bowls of food and...licks them.
12. Door Sniffer, who has a huge nose, and loves stealing baked goods.
13. Candle Beggar, who steals sweets.

Considering they're supposed to cast some judgment on the behavior of the little children of Iceland, there's a lot of thieving and strange licking going on...

THE GREAT LUTE DEFENSE

Some strategic moves in military history are so brazen and courageous that one can't help but feel impressed. Think of the famous Trojan horse, a masterful act of deception whereby a "gift" was wheeled into the gates of Troy, seemingly as an olive branch of peace, but in fact containing a battalion of soldiers who hopped out at night and killed the sleeping Trojans. Masterful, though the plan was based on the Trojans not being very bright and not checking the horse's door to see what was inside.

A remarkably impertinent strategy was on display several centuries later during the wars of the Han Dynasty in China. The strategy was known as the Empty Fort Strategy and was supposedly carried out a few times by different generals to varying degrees of success. The basic idea goes that one employs some reverse psychology when an invading army looks certain to beat your force.

The General orders the soldiers to either hide or flee from the fort, lowering all flags and removing siege weaponry with haste. Once this is done, the gates are opened for the invaders as they come near. In theory, the invading force will be unsure of how to proceed given the unusual sight before them and may in fact not invade at all.

Supposedly the great tactician Zhuge Liang employed this tactic to great effect when he held a small garrison of 100 troops at a fort, under attack from rival war master Sima Yi. The latter boasted a force of some 15,000 and would have had no problem with devastating the small army cowering in the fort. Zhuge Liang decided to employ a version of the Empty Fort Strategy and ordered all of his soldiers to hide as he ascended the wall to look out over Sima Yi's approaching forces. Liang pulled out a lute and began playing.

The soldiers were shaken, and Sima Yi was convinced that an elaborate trap was in play. Liang looked far too comfortable for a general who was likely about to die and it was unnerving. Sima Yi pulled his forces back to consider what awaited them and how best to proceed. The strategy worked and Liang managed to avoid what would have been a complete slaughter.

HILARIOUS!
YOU'RE KILLING ME!

There are those times in life, rarer in adult years, unfortunately, where you are laughing so very much that for a moment you genuinely can't catch your breath. Children experience it quite a bit as they roll around in fits of laughter at whatever joyful thing has set their hearts alight; adults do get it for a moment but then remember the crushing futility of life and soon stop. This moment of "stop" didn't quite happen for Chrysippus, an Ancient Greek philosopher who lived from 279–206 BCE.

Chrysippus remains a respected Stoic philosopher and one of the most formative thinkers in the influential school of thought. He spoke about the ethics of human behavior, physics, and how humans can employ their logic to better understand the universe and their place within it. A very smart man indeed.

Though a smart man, Chrysippus proved that death will come for us all in whatever way it wants - our intelligence may not have any part to play when it comes to the closing of the final curtain. He was 73 at the time of his death and there exists two accounts of his death from Diogenes, who wrote on the topic.

Either Chrysippus died from being too drunk at a feast, or he watched a donkey eating figs (already a hilarious sight, we've all been there) and proclaimed that someone should give the mule some wine to wash down the figs. He then proceeded to *literally* die from laughter. Chrysippus supposedly failed to gain his breath back and died with no air from his lungs as he howled at a bemused donkey.

Yep, he went out on a joke about giving a donkey some wine. It wasn't even a good joke! Smart dude but what a rubbish sense of humor. He wouldn't last a minute at the Comedy Club in London.

IF ONLY THERE WAS
A HYDRANT NEARBY

In the world of copyright infringement and intellectual property theft, patents have become rather important things. A patent is essentially a bit of paper you get to certify that "this idea is mine" and no one else can use it without your say-so. Obtaining a patent isn't always easy; you have to prove that it's purely your idea, feasible, and not copying someone else. For instance, walking into the office holding a Kiwi fruit you've painted purple isn't going to get a patent. But proving the concept for a pair of roller skates that also feed you a strawberry milkshake might…, that's not a bad idea, actually.

It's also fun to browse patents, just to see what people are coming up with out there. Some are terrifying. For instance, Sony has patented a form of technology that means the adverts on your television stop playing if you're not literally *looking* at them. Some patents are downright silly like a Moustache Guard patented in 1876. If there's one thing that needs protecting it's the 'tache. Not the nose though, just the 'tache.

Unfortunately, a great amount of historical information was lost in 1836 when the US Patent Office caught fire and all records inside the building were lost in a fiery blaze. Some suspected that it was arson, potentially by a man furious that his invention of a double-ended spoon was refused for patenting, but it was likely an accident.

Thousands of dollars were spent to attempt to re-create the burned-up forms from partial fragments left behind after the inferno, but only about a quarter was recovered (even after spending some $100,000 on doing so). Ironically, in the office was the patent for the fire hydrant, now seen around North America on most street corners. The hydrant allows access to a large amount of water quickly to help firefighters battle serious fires with the greatest number of resources at their disposal. Unfortunately, however, no one had yet installed one by the

218

Patent Offices, and the patent was lost in the fire. So, we don't know *who* invented the hydrant, we just know that if the idea had been installed on a grander scale, then it could have helped prevent the inventor's patent from going up in flames, possibly making them rather famous and rich. Instead, they made basically nothing from their revolutionary design. Sometimes life just isn't fair, no matter how bright you are.

SOMEONE IN HERE IS
A SPY, ANY IDEAS?

Would you spy on your employer for $1.4 million? Many people probably would; some people would do it for a Snickers bar and a high-five.

In effect, this was the question posed to Agent Robert Hanssen during the 1970s, 80s, and 90s. Admittedly, no one offered him the option of doing this, he sought it out himself. Hanssen was an FBI agent, joining in 1976, during a time of great international tension. Three years after he joined, he offered his services to the Soviet Main Intelligence Directorate.

Ultimately, throughout his career, Hanssen engaged in three different periods of divulging top-secret information to the Russian secret service: from 1979–1981, 1985–1991, and from 1992-2001. Hanssen passed on information about what the US was planning to do in case of nuclear war, new munitions developments, and aspects of the US intelligence service.

Embarrassingly, while in the bureau Hanssen was tasked to sift out any potential KGB agents who may be spying on American intelligence. Hanssen's work led to the unearthing of several agents, many of whom were executed for betraying the United States of America. It wasn't until Aldrich Ames was apprehended in 1994 and exposed many of the intelligence breaches that the Bureau began to suspect Hanssen of espionage at all. Hanssen had worked hard to remain anonymous to the Russian government, knowing it would be dangerous to divulge too much. However, the FBI made links with a KGB agent who it was thought may have had some contact with American spies. They paid the agent $7 million and the agent in turn provided them with a file about an "anonymous mole," which contained enough information to point the finger firmly at Hanssen.

The American traitor was arrested in 2001 and was sentenced to 15 consecutive life sentences without any possibility of parole for betraying America. The Department of Justice described the whole incident as:

"Possibly the worst intelligence disaster in U.S. history."

Hanssen must have been kicking himself when he found out that a KGB agent ratted him out for $7 million while he worked tirelessly for 22 years for a little over $1 million.

THE MASKED MARAUDERS

What if, in the 1960s, you were told that a top-secret album had just been recorded by a supergroup containing John Lennon, Mick Jagger, Bob Dylan, Paul McCartney, George Harrison, and more guest appearances from the legends of the Rock 'n' Roll scene? You'd have been gob smacked - you'd *need* that album! Hell, if it was released today, you'd *need* that album, and not only because two of the main contributors are dead.

Well, read a couple of excerpts from this review from a 1969 copy of *Rolling Stone* magazine of an album titled *The Masked Marauders*:

> "*Dylan shines on Side Three, displaying his new deep bass voice, with 'Duke of Earl'.*"

> "*The LP opens with an eighteen-minute version of 'Season of the Witch'. The cut is highlighted by an amazing jam between bass and piano, both played by Paul McCartney.*"

> "*It can truly be said that this album is more than a way of life; it is life.*"

If you know your music, you might be able to tell that this review is laughing at the reader's expense, and you'd be right. *The Masked Marauders*, unfortunately, doesn't exist. Well, it does. Just not as has been described.

The review from *Rolling Stone* magazine was the first part of an expertly crafted prank. The review was glowing, describing the album as an absolute must-have for any true music fan. After its publication, *Rolling Stone* received an overwhelming amount of correspondence, demanding to know how to get hold of the incredible-sounding album. Interestingly enough, both Allen Klein, the manager of the Rolling Stones and The Beatles, and Albert Grossman, manager of Bob Dylan, also enquired.

On to stage two then, to record the album. The editor Langdon Winner hired a minor band called the Cleanliness and Godliness Skiffle Band to record for radio broadcast the three songs that were mentioned by name in the review. They recorded the tracks, pretending to be some of the world's best-known musicians and all watched on as the songs were broadcast across Los Angeles and San Francisco. Warner Bros won the rights to record the full album, jumping on the hype that the album had gained through an entirely falsified review. They also signed the band to a record deal.

The record spent 12 weeks in the charts, peaking at no. 114 and achieving modern cult status as a brilliant prank that went, as all pranks should, too far and exactly far enough. If you're interested, you can pick the vinyl up for a cheap price today because the album wasn't made by any genius songwriters, so is terrible.

YOU REALLY ARE QUITE THE ASSASSIN, AREN'T YOU?

Many people know how World War I started. In the words of the show *Blackadder*:

"A guy called Archie Duke shot an ostrich because he was hungry."

Or: "The Archduke of the Austro-Hungarian Empire called Franz Ferdinand was shot." There's a lot more behind the outbreak of World War I in 1914, but ultimately, the execution of the archduke led to a domino effect of countries declaring war. The execution itself was carried out by a Serbian nationalist group called The Black Hand Gang with Gavrilo Princip firing the fatal bullet at Franz Ferdinand after a botched assassination attempt mere hours earlier in the day.

Princip's story is relatively well known. The Archduke was visiting Sarajevo, Bosnia in an open-top car so he might wave at the crowds of people looking on. Assassination attempts with bombs and guns had failed earlier in the day and, certain that he'd be found out, Princip had escaped from the streets to a nearby bakery to purchase a sandwich. He ate it, happening to exit the shop as the Archduke's car pulled up outside the shop. Princip shot the Archduke and his wife, and that was that.

While his story is one of bizarre, grim luck with a smidgeon of humor, the truly hilarious story comes from before the Archduke was killed when another member of the gang called Nedeljko Čabrinović had his opportunity to kill the unpopular royal.

As Ferdinand's motorcade drove past, Čabrinović threw a bomb at the car that had been designed by a weapons expert in the Serbian army. With a direct impact, the car would completely explode, leaving no one with a half chance of survival. However, Čabrinović forgot about the 10-second detonator, so the bomb bounced off the car and blew up the vehicle behind the Archduke!

Sensing that he may be about to be caught and tortured for his rubbish murder, Čabrinović swallowed some arsenic that the group had procured to kill themselves with should they need to. He decided to give himself no chance by also hurling himself to the bottom of the river which ran alongside the motorcade, ensuring that he would die a martyr rather than be taken in and tortured. Regrettably, the river was four inches deep where he jumped in, and the arsenic was old and didn't work properly. Čabrinović was slowly pulled out of the river as the crowd looked on, rolling their eyes, and he was taken into custody. He was tortured and asked for more information on the co-conspirators, which he gladly gave over to save his own life.

Cold-blooded killer? Not quite. Complete moron? Perhaps.

AND THERE'S NO BIG HAT EMPORIUM AROUND HERE?

You'll have heard of the infamous Blackbeard by now (if not, then clearly you haven't read the whole book yet. Or you've forgotten it all, which is as useless as not reading it in the first place - go on, go back and read it). Edward Teach was his real name and he was a rightfully feared pirate who took whatever he needed, including people's lives if he felt like it.

As fearsome as he was, he learned a lot of this pirating "skill" from another pirate called Benjamin Hornigold. Teach was Hornigold's second in command by the mid-1710s and saw firsthand how a pirate made their mark. Between the two of them, by 1717 they had amassed a fleet of stolen ships that quickly became the most powerful force in the Bahamas. Hornigold selected his weapons with glee, and his sailors carefully, looking for a vindictive and violent glint in their eyes.

Though brutal and effective, Hornigold and Teach showed an odd streak of humor in their work. In 1717, they attacked a merchant ship near Honduras. Those on board weren't fighters and could barely keep the pirates at bay for a minute before they surrendered their vessel to the thieves. The captain begged Hornigold not to kill them, to take what they desired but to spare their lives at least. Hornigold politely explained that they had no desire to kill, nor indeed to take much - the crew had simply gotten drunk the night before and thrown their hats into the sea. They now requested the hats of the merchants. The merchants did in fact give the pirate crew their hats and they were permitted to simply sail away, as though completely uninterrupted by the meeting.

Hornigold's crew mutinied late in the year and Blackbeard was unable to prevent the betrayal. Hornigold handed himself over to the British government and worked as a pirate hunter, hunting his old associates such as Blackbeard. He failed to catch his old friend and after a serious crash in 1718 around the Bahamas, he was never seen again.

THE POETRY OF
MRS. SILENCE DOGOOD

Death is a fisherman, the world we see
His fish-pond is, and we the fishes be;
His net some general sickness; howe'er he
Is not so kind as other fishers be;
For if they take one of the smaller fry,
They throw him in again, he shall not die:
But death is sure to kill all he can get,
And all is fish with him that comes to net.

If you haven't read any of Mrs. Silence Dogood's poetry before, you have now. A nice analogous reading that reads quite well and was published in 1722.

Mrs. Dogood became a published poet in the *New England Courant*, a newspaper founded by James Franklin, the brother of the famous polymath Benjamin Franklin. The paper was printed out of Boston. Dogood never met James Franklin; instead, she communicated entirely by letters that were left under the door of the printing shop once every two weeks. The first letter started:

"Sir,

It may not be possible in the first Place to inform your Readers, that I intend once a
Fortnight to present them, by the Help of this Paper, with a short Epistle, which I
presume will add somewhat to their Entertainment."

That's the confident assuredness of a woman who knew that her poetry was worth reading and worth publishing! Her poems were published every two weeks along with her writings and musings and her name gained recognition for the ability, humor, and intelligence of her work.

There's just one thing - Mrs. Silence Dogood was actually Benjamin Franklin. Benjamin Franklin was, at the time of publication, only 16 years old and had worked in his brother's printing house for a while as an apprentice. He showed his brother some of his work, but James was remarkably callous, giving his brother no quarter and deeming his work unprintable. Benjamin knew that his work was at least decent enough for publication so adopted the pseudonym "Mrs. Silence Dogood" and created a whole backstory and new set of work for her.

Dogood was a middle-aged widow who had experienced life's hardship through the early death of her father, the unfortunate demise of her husband, and the miserable departure of her mother. All of it was, of course, made up.

Eventually, James must have found out. Perhaps he would have been annoyed, but it would serve to be just one story in the hundreds about Benjamin Franklin and his remarkable ability to do pretty much anything he desired (apart from gymnastics; he wasn't so great at that).

AROUND THE
WORLD IN 169 DAYS

Around the World in 80 Days was published in 1873 and made a dramatic impact on the world of entertainment in the Western world. Many movies have been made (and likely, will be made) of the epic story, alongside stage productions and, best of all, challenges inspired by the novel. One such challenge was the 1908 New York to Paris Race, which was seen as a true test of the top-of-the-range automobiles and their longevity.

Six contestants attempted the race and three made it across the finish line in Paris with the American team winning in a now-famous Thomas Flyer car, currently on display at the National Automobile Museum in Reno, Nevada. The race started in Time Square, New York City on February 12, 1908. The cars set off at the sound of a gunshot. There were three French teams, with Germany, Italy, and the US having a team each.

It took 41 days for the Thomas Flyer to make it to San Francisco. The route to San Francisco was impressive. The cars were driving on very few paved roads and often resorted to attempting to drive on locomotive tracks (perhaps they cheated and simply tied a rope *to* the locomotive, we'll never truly know). The teams had settled into a routine of waking up by 5 a.m. and sleeping by 8 p.m., allowing their mechanics to make constant and necessary repairs to the vehicles so they could continue through the harsh winter. The trip from New York to San Francisco also made history as the first automobile journey across the United States of America in winter.

It is unsurprising to learn that the next destination, Alaska, was impossible for the cars to drive in. Even in the 2020s, many cars struggle with the conditions of Alaska, and now the state is far better set up for cars. The organizers decided to reroute through Japan and

Vladivostok, Siberia to begin crossing the continents of Asia and Europe.

Throughout the Siberian leg, progress was exceptionally slow, and the cars were being measured in feet per hour rather than miles per hour for many of the wetter sections. There was *no* infrastructure in the region (there's even less nowadays), and it was almost impossible to drive the early automobiles without some sort of road underneath them.

The Thomas Flyer arrived in Paris on July 30, 1908, having covered a staggering 9,941 miles. The journey still holds the record for the longest automotive competition in terms of time taken. The crew was stopped near the finish line by a policeman who'd spotted that they had no headlamps on their car. He would hear no excuses about the race; after all, the law was the law. Luckily, a passing cyclist decided to stop and pop his lightbulbs into the car, and so they were on their way. The Germans had actually arrived four days earlier but had been penalized a full 30 days as they'd taken trains and boats for approximately a third of the overall trip. "It's just efficient."

Along the way, the other teams complained of cheating, particularly from the Americans. Across the American strait, the civilians were charging the foreign teams for sleeping on the floor, over-charging them for petrol or sometimes just telling them they had none. The competition was fierce, and the teams complained about the boorishness of the Americans and their lack of good graces or manners. Sounds much the same as in the 21st century.

YOU HAVE THE RIGHT
TO REMAIN SILENT. WHICH
YOU'RE DOING VERY WELL.

The phrase "flogging a dead horse" has been overused for the last century. We should replace it with something that means the same thing but is different. Honestly, it's like "flogging a dead horse!" How about "putting a dead man on trial"?

This is exactly what happened in January 897 CE in Rome as the deceased Pope Formosus was tried for perjury by Pope Stephen VI.

Formosus had been dead for approximately seven months by the time he was put on trial. Stephen VI ordered that Formosus' corpse be removed from Saint Peter's Basilica, and the rotting cadaver was propped up on a throne in the papal court. Formosus was assigned a deacon to answer on his behalf, for which he showed no gratitude whatsoever.

Why Stephen VI felt the need to put the body of Formosus on trial is disputed by historians and finding a straightforward reason is difficult. It was almost certainly a political move. Essentially, Formosus had crowned Lambert the co-ruler of the Holy Roman Empire, alongside Lambert's father Guy III. Formosus didn't like Guy so invited Arnulf to invade and take the crown of the Empire for himself in 892. Arnulf failed in his invasion but re-ignited his attempts in 895 shortly following the death of Guy III. Arnulf succeeded and Formosus crowned him as the Emperor. Both Formosus and Arnulf died shortly after the crowning and that was that. The problem is deciphering exactly why Stephen VI hated Formosus' actions so much. Stephen likely had political alliances that he needed to support.

The outcome is not surprising: the corpse was found guilty. His speech was atrocious, after all. Stephen formally invalidated all of Formosus' actions and announced that his papacy was null. Formosus was reburied but was eventually removed from his grave (without checking with him) and thrown into the Tiber River.

Doesn't seem like a particularly holy action by either pope, but the idea of berating a corpse is inherently silly and quite funny.

AGENT SNUGGLES, REPORTING FOR MILK—I MEAN DUTY

We've considered a few quite bonkers ideas from intelligence agencies already in this book, mainly assassination attempts on world leaders. It's fun to imagine what you would try to do given an almost infinite budget as head of the CIA or some such organization. How bizarrely would you act to get one over on your adversaries? Perhaps, teach a baboon how to operate a sniper rifle? Instruct a grouse on how to win a by-election in mainland Europe? Direct an orange to lead a world economy? There are countless possibilities, and it can be quite fun to speculate.

This logic seems to be what led the CIA to launch an outlandish project to spy on Soviet embassies. Some bright spark had the idea of using *cats* to spy. Cats, you know, the animals that are renowned for doing their own thing and not giving much of a care for what you, the human, want.

An unfortunate cat was chosen, and a veterinary surgeon spent an hour implanting a microphone in the moggy's ear, alongside a radio transmitter at the base of its skull with a wire into its fur. This was to allow the cat to record conversations while transmitting them back to whoever was listening. The project was dubbed "Acoustic Kitty," though the more elegant solution would have been to have given the cat security clearance and dub it "Agent Snuggles."

The cat's first mission was to listen into a conversation that two men were engaged in outside of the Soviet Embassy in Washington D.C. The cat was surreptitiously released and Agent Snuggles set about his important task. The account goes that Snuggles deftly, quietly, and with great poise ran in front of a taxi and died.

In 2013, it was denied that the cat died instantly. The CIA maintained that at $20 million, the project was too expensive, and cats were just too unruly to adequately train to make the mission viable. It was

234

cancelled in 1967 regardless and disclosed only in 2001 with the declassification of some documents. The thing is though, the CIA *would* say that it was simply too expensive, because the other story is just so embarrassing.

Who knows, we may find out that throughout the '90s, foxes were hacking into databases while hedgehogs were acting as pin cushions to spy on the cartel in Mexico.

BORIS YELTSIN'S LATE-NIGHT PIZZA

If you weren't around in the mid-90s - or were around but not old enough to understand anything greater than where you can get dessert, when you will get dessert, and what is the dessert - then you may not know who Boris Yeltsin was.

Boris Yeltsin was the Russian leader after the Soviet Union had ended and with it, the Cold War. The new era of Russian-American politics was now upon us and not a moment too soon - the decades of intense, aggressive threatening had to end for the safety of the world. Yeltsin was on interesting terms with Bill Clinton, the US President; they certainly didn't seem to despise one another. Yeltsin famously gifted Clinton a pair of hockey jerseys with the words "Yeltsin 96" and "'Clinton 96" on the back and reduced Clinton to tears of laughter after dubbing the United States press "a disaster" at a joint press conference.

Yeltsin is well known for being an avid consumer of alcohol also, something which undoubtedly led to his demise and crumbling reputation by the end of his presidency.

In 1994, the two leaders met in Washington for the first time, but the more shocking details of their meetings weren't well publicized until the late 2000s, likely because of how embarrassing it was. Yeltsin had indulged in his fair share of alcohol while in Washington and somehow managed to escape onto Pennsylvania Avenue in the night. Secret Service agents found him barely able to speak, in his underwear, and screaming for a taxi to take him to pizza.

Clinton later revealed that Yeltsin did, indeed, get his pizza.

CONCLUSION

That's your lot: your 127 stories which display some of the oddest and best across human (and sometimes animal) history. If you've read all of it diligently, then you'll have read incredible stories about unsinkable cats, Benjamin Franklin's oddities, cannibal pioneers, and the secret formula to winning every horse race (you didn't read that!? You must have missed it, it's in there, promise).

With any luck you've been in a space that is well suited for laughter as you've perused this silly collection, such as the toilet or your sofa. With the greatest of respects, reading it while at a funeral will likely be frowned upon (though may provide a funny enough story for the sequel, so do let us know). And with even greater luck, you've enjoyed it. The annuls of history provide incredible reading and, hopefully, you are feeling inspired enough to dig a little deeper into the stories behind the stories.

History is a wonderful subject to indulge oneself in - it shouldn't just be reserved for the classroom or the coffee-stained offices of an old university building. Whichever stories you enjoyed the most will likely have some interesting context behind them. Why did a comedian create a fake society for clothing animals? Why do so many popes have eccentric stories attached to them? Go and read, Google, watch, or listen to as much history as you can; it will surely only enrich your life.

If you feel compelled to, then tell others about the hilarious stories you've read on these pages and, ideally, tell them to get hold of their own copy so they can read more. Regardless, share the love of learning, while simultaneously securing your spot in the team for the next quiz night. If you can rattle off Winston Churchill's daily routine, you'll look very clever and will be in line to win the $65 gift voucher for you and your pals.

Otherwise, all we have left to say is thank you for reading this collection of 127 stories. We hope you had fun and saw it as a worthwhile use of your precious hours on Earth. Now why don't you get out there and create some stories yourself? Who knows, maybe a book will be published a few years from now with your crazy life inside of it...